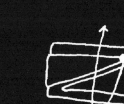

Onigiri

*Japanese
rice balls
made easy!*

おにぎり

**AI WATANABE
& SAMUEL TRIFOT**

PHOTOGRAPHY BY
Akiko Ida

Contents

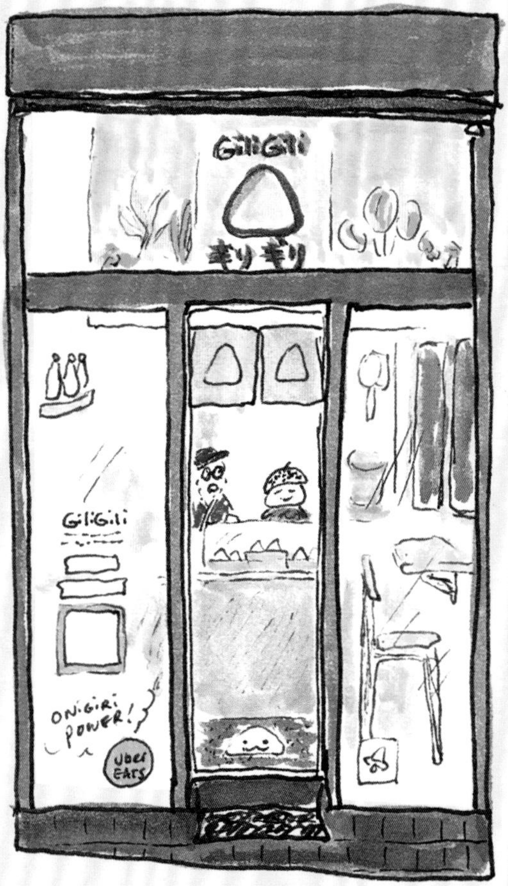

GiliGili
ONIGIRI POWER!

ABOUT

FISH

VEGGIES

MEAT

SOUP, SNACKS & PICKLED FOOD

Gili-Gili!

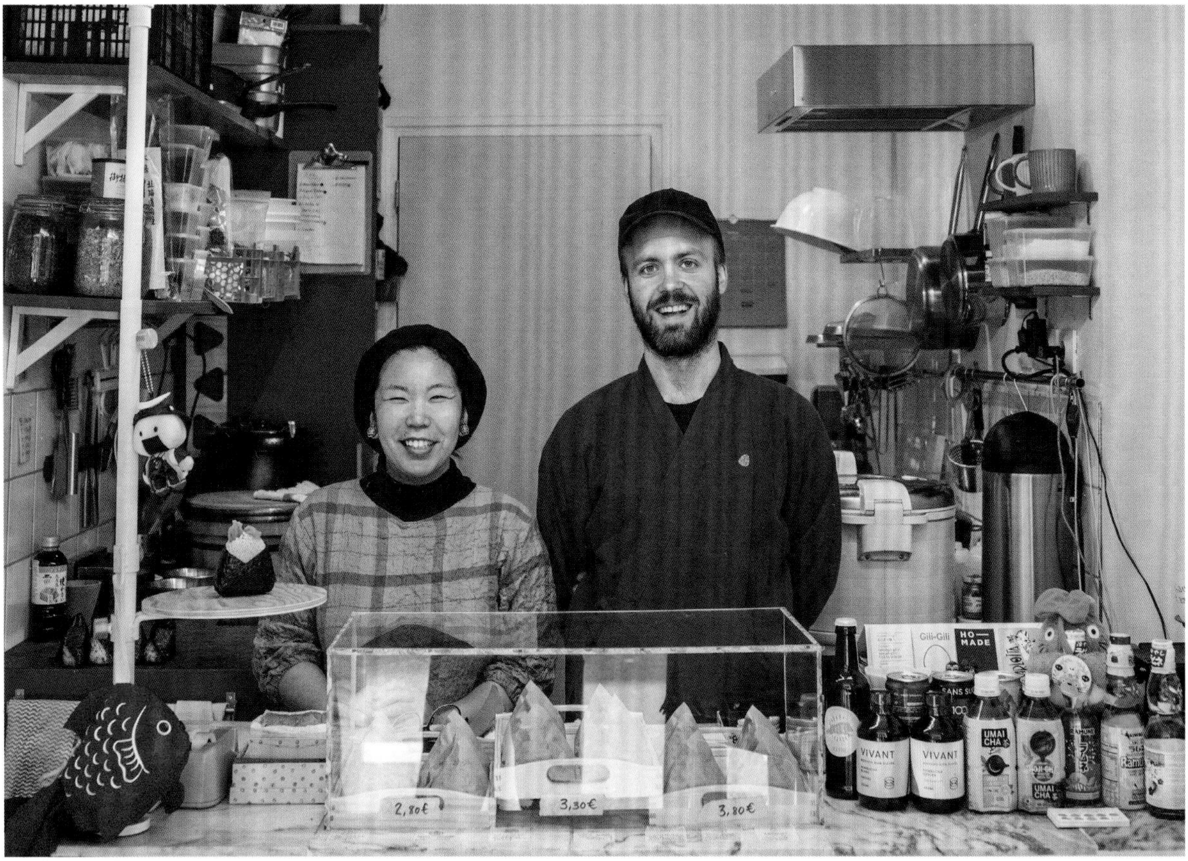
2,80€
3,30€
3,80€
VIVANT
VIVANT
UMAI CHA
Gili-Gili
HO-MADE

A SMALL HISTORY LESSON

In spring 2018, on the traditional Hina Matsuri holiday (the Japanese festival of dolls for girls), we hosted an onigiri workshop in Le Pavillon des Canaux in Paris, which is what ultimately led us to create Gili-Gili. From the moment our adventure began, and even from the first moment we had the idea of opening a restaurant, we wanted to pass on and share our passion for onigiri. Today, we're very proud to say that we have been given the opportunity to publicize this millennia-old Japanese snack to a large number of people thanks to this book.

PASSION FOR ONIGIRI

Every time we were out and about in Japan, onigiri was the snack we'd bring with us because it's simple, healthy, economical, practical, and consistent. And to our dismay, every time we came back to France, we would notice that there was a clear lack of onigiri in the Japanese and Asian restaurants and stores of Paris, especially when compared to its distant cousin: sushi. Japanese gastronomy is so rich and beautiful that we decided to become onigiri ambassadors in France—through Gili-Gili!

LOCAL AND SEASONAL PRODUCTS

Throughout this book, we offer you simple, straightforward recipes and suggest you use seasonal products as much encourage you to purchase fresh and local ingredients (for example, substitute wasabi with horseradish).

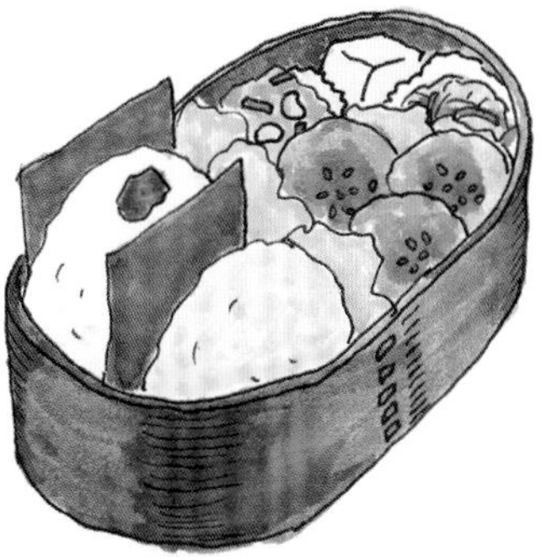

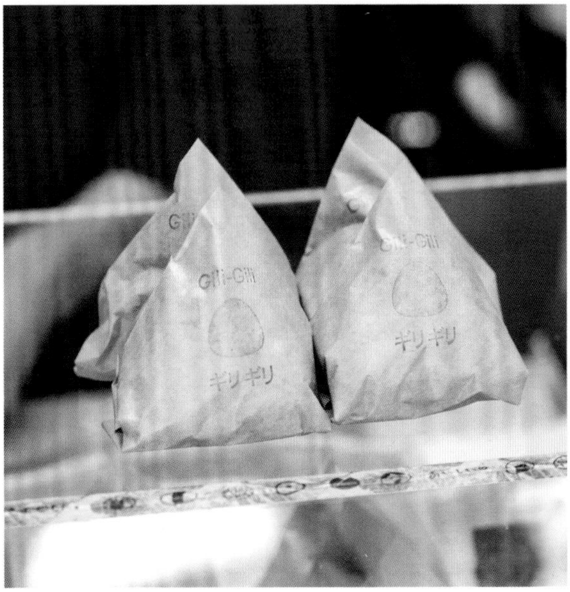
ギリギリ
ギリギリ

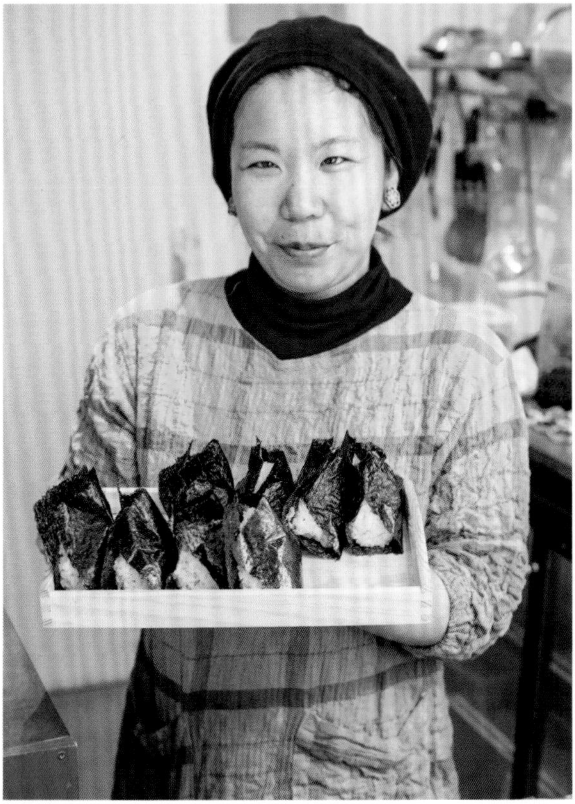

JAPANESE SOUL FOOD

Soul food is the term used in Japan to describe this stuffed rice ball that greatly energizes both mind and body. When making an onigiri by hand, the cook, through direct contact with the rice ball, passes on their best to the person who eats the onigiri.

The one piece of advice we received the most from all the onigiri specialists we met in Japan was to make onigiri with love, and that is exactly what we do in our store on 48 rue Notre Dame de Lorette in Paris, France.

We hope you'll find a ton of joy in discovering, making, and experiencing this little triangle that only means well.

What Is an Onigiri?

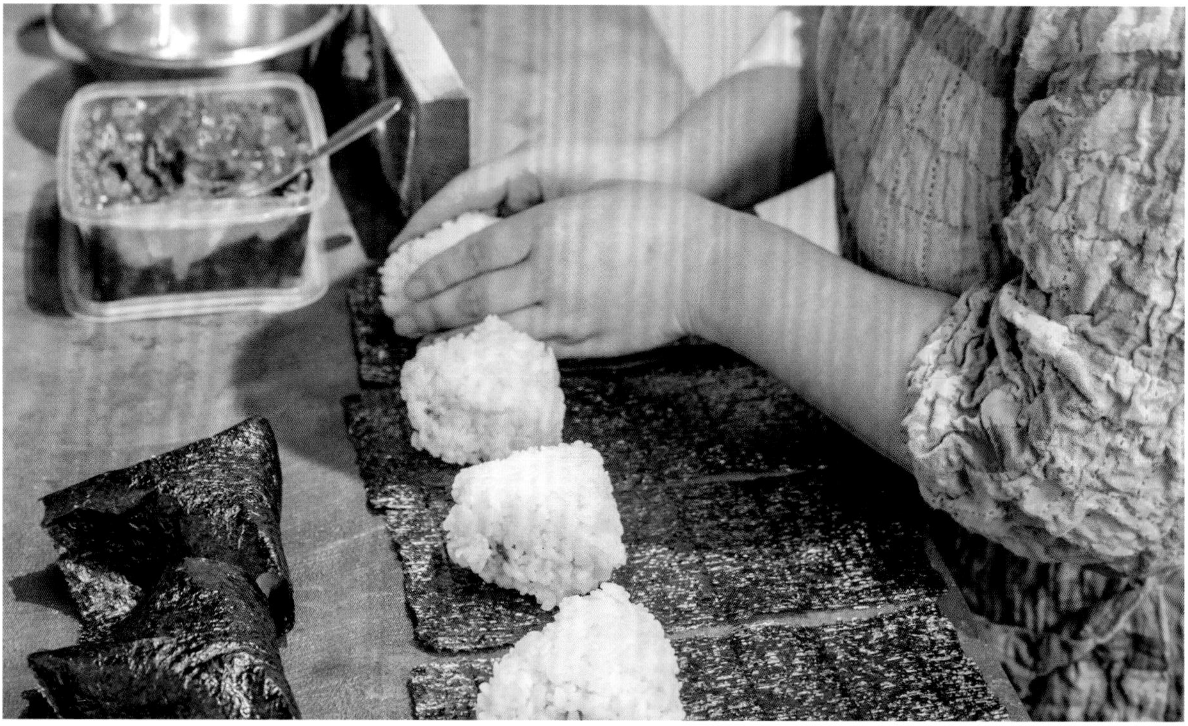

A POPULAR SNACK

Fans of will surely know a little about this triangular, slightly salted ball of rice, which is stuffed with a seemingly infinite variety of fillings and, more often than not, clothed in a sheet of *nori* seaweed (which can be eaten crispy or soft, depending on preference).

The onigiri (also referred to as *omusubi* in certain regions) comes in various shapes—ball-shaped, triangular, flattened round, or square—and with a variety of garnishes. It can be eaten both hot and cold. It's rich in fiber, sodium, and carbohydrates, yet low in calories: 150 to 200 kilocalories, depending on the garnish. It's easily digestible and regulates appetite.

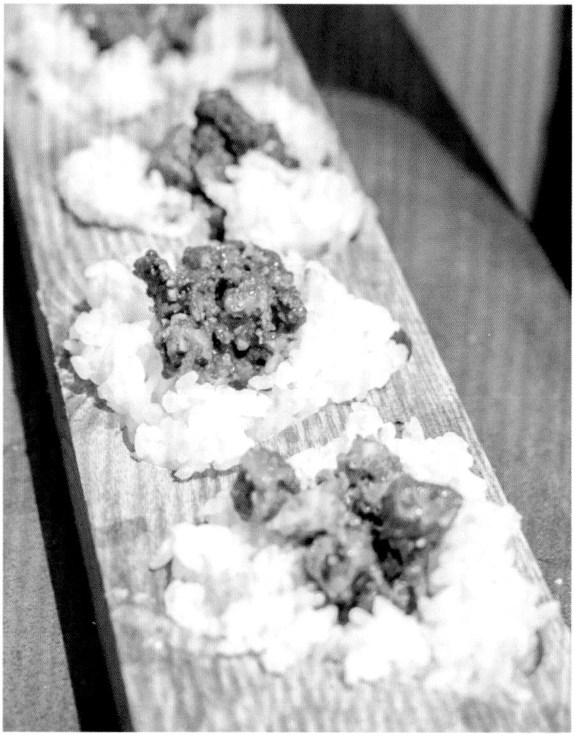

That's why you can eat onigiri at any time of day, and why it's so prominently available in Japanese *konbini*, convenience stores that are often open 24-7. It is said that one out of ten Japanese people eats an onigiri each day!

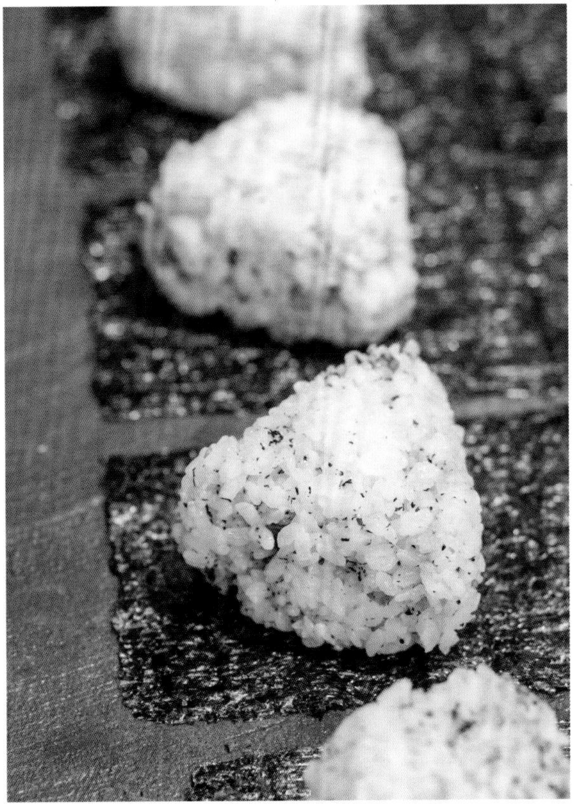

GOOD FOR HUMANKIND AND THE PLANET

Onigiri is a long-lasting snack that is eco-friendly and eco-conscious, which meets certain modern challenges.

It's **inclusive**: it fits any alimentary lifestyle and is enjoyed by people of all ages.

It's **cheap** to make.

It's made with local rice, and the water used for the rice can be **recycled**.

For the packaging, ***furoshiki***, a traditional Japanese packaging fabric, can be used, so there are no plastics or dishwashing involved.

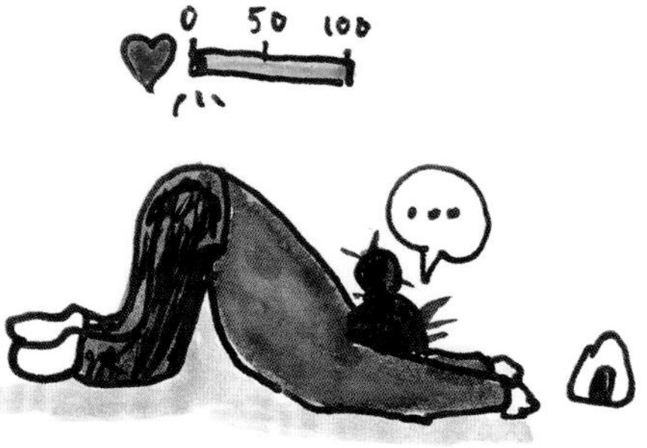
0 50 100

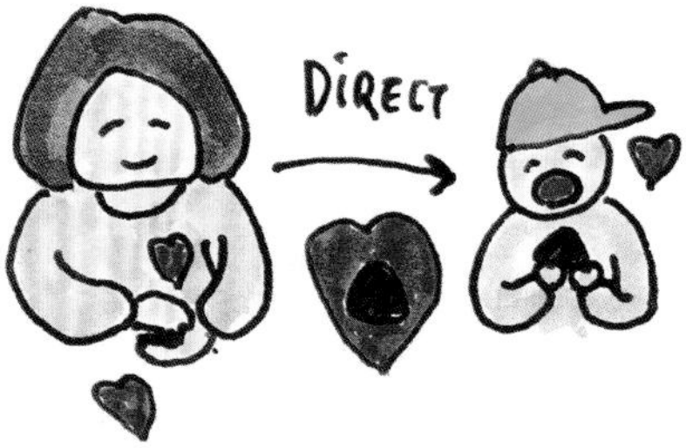
DIRECT

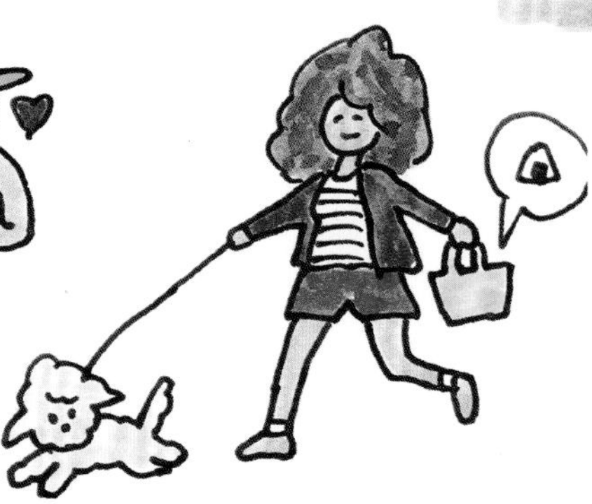

Throughout History

YAYOI PERIOD: TENTH CENTURY BCE TO MID-THIRD CENTURY CE

The earliest record of onigiri is from a fossil found on the historical site of Sugitani Chanobatake in Ishikawa Prefecture. Along with being a portable source of sustenance, it's likely that onigiri was seen as an offering to the gods or even as a tool to ward off evil spirits. We believe its triangular shape comes from the superstition that gods would come down to earth from the top of the onigiri, like descending a mountain.

KOFUN PERIOD: THIRD CENTURY TO SEVENTH CENTURY

Paleontologists have discovered a fossilized onigiri *bento*, or Japanese boxed lunch, on the historical site of Kitagawahyō in the city of Yokohama, dating from the end of the sixth century. This *bento* was found in basket form and was filled with several large piles of whole-grain rice.

KAMAKURA PERIOD: 1185 TO 1333

During the Jōkyū rebellion instigated by the Retired Emperor Go-Toba, the shogunate's forces emerged victorious. This was the first time in the history of Japan that the shogunate gained the upper hand politically over the imperial court. During their battles, the shogunate warriors were handed onigiri garnished with *umeboshi*, salted Japanese plums (perhaps to help the warriors stay fit thanks to the *umeboshi*'s antibacterial effect or the glucose contained in the rice). This is how *umeboshi* became known all around the country.

EDO PERIOD: 1603 TO 1868

By now, onigiri had reached even the general populace, who would regularly eat it when on the road or during work in the fields. This is also why it was referenced in the popular tale "Saru Kani Gassen" (The Crab and the Monkey), and it was even portrayed in one of the prints of the ukiyo-e series *The Fifty-Three Stations of the Tōkaidō*, by the artist Hiroshige. The cultivation of *nori* seaweed started in the bay of Tokyo during the second half of the seventeenth century, which brought with it the first sightings of the *nori*-wrapped onigiri.

MEIJI ERA: 1868 TO 1912

In 1885, the first *ekiben*, a type of *bento* sold in train stations, made their appearance at Utsunomiya Station in Tochigi Prefecture. They consisted of onigiri filled with *umeboshi* and sprinkled with Japanese

sesame salt, also known as *gomashio*. In 1889, the Yamagata Prefecture private school Chūai Elementary began—for the first time in Japan—to offer a canteen service for children of disadvantaged families. The dish served consisted of onigiri and grilled salmon.

SHŌWA ERA: 1926 TO 1989

In 1978, the 7-Eleven *konbini* chain (small grocery stores open 24-7) launched the first onigiri sold in new packaging separating the rice from the *nori*. This innovation, called *paritto shiki* (meaning "the crispy method") was an overwhelming success.

In 1983, the same chain of *konbini* started offering tuna-mayo onigiri. For one hundred years, the top-selling onigiri garnishes had always been *umeboshi* and *kombu* kelp, leaving no space for any new recipes, but tuna-mayo soon took the market by storm and is still, to this day, the most popular onigiri sold across all Japanese *konbini*.

HEISEI ERA: 1989 TO 2019

In 2014, the rise of the so-called *onigirazu* began. This type of onigiri is not shaped. It was first introduced in 1991 in volume 22 of the Japanese cooking manga *Cooking Papa*, but it owes its rise in popularity to its appearance on the cooking site Cookpad.

Then in 2018, *akuma no onigiri* (the onigiri of the devil) experienced an extraordinary boom. Originally, this recipe was the work of a chef who was part of a Japanese Antarctic expedition team and wanted to utilize their leftovers. The recipe was then featured on Japanese television as an onigiri garnish associated with the expedition, creating unprecedented buzz on the Japanese web.

The *konbini* chain Lawson then commercialized the recipe under the name it is now known by, *akuma no onigiri*. It became so popular it nearly dethroned the king of onigiri, the tuna-mayo onigiri.

A NEW CRAZE

Not too long ago, Pierre Hermé declared that the era of sushi will also be the era of onigiri in the gastronomy magazine *Dancyu*. June 18 is now known as Onigiri Day in Japan. This is the day that the oldest fossil of an onigiri, dating back 2,000 years to the Yayoi era, was found.

The Perfect Rice

The rice used to make onigiri is the short-grain white rice known as the *japonica* variety. It is naturally sweet and rich in starch, and its grains stick to one another.

....

Its ability to absorb tremendous amounts of water when boiling gives it an elastic and soft texture, along with a certain luster that varies depending on the quality of the rice. This rice can be found in large supermarkets or Asian grocery stores. It is sometimes sold under the moniker of "sushi rice." In a pinch, you can also use risotto or arborio rice.

....

Along with the rice, we recommend using high-quality salt and either filtered water or water purified with activated *binchōtan** charcoal.

Short-grain rice—like all its fellow rice varieties—can be conserved in a hermetically sealed container as long as it is kept safe from air, light, and heat. It's gluten-free, so it works well for people with a gluten intolerance.

*Binchōtan originates from an *ubamegashi* oak wood in the south of Japan. It's an activated charcoal that notably gets rid of chlorine and certain organic micropollutants.

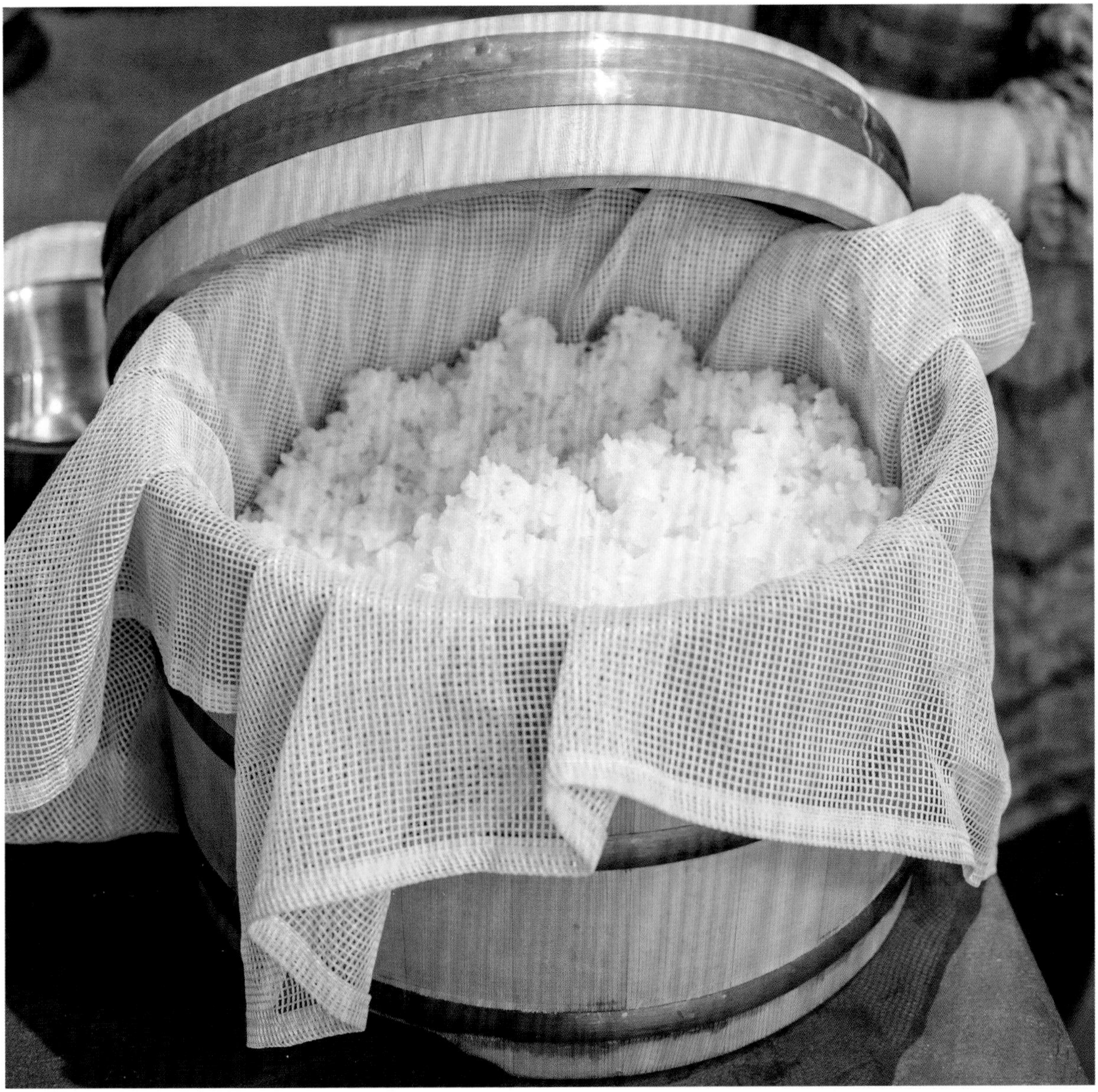

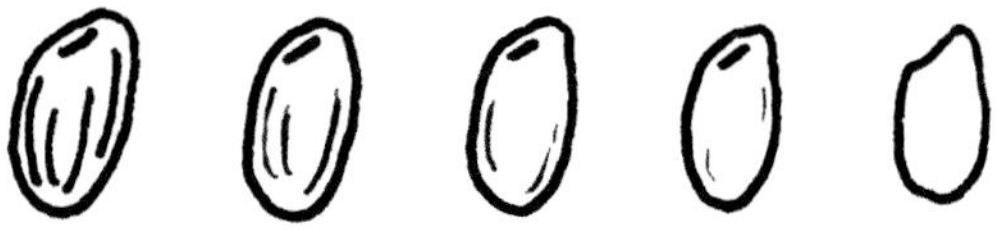

Fun fact! Did you know that the annual consumption of rice in Japan has dropped by 50 percent in the last fifty years? It went from 260.8 pounds (118.3 kilograms) per capita in 1963 to 120.4 pounds (54.6 kilograms) per capita in 2015. In France, the consumption peaks around 5 kilograms, or around 11 pounds, per capita!

Cooking the Rice

There are many ways to cook rice. The most common way involves using a saucepan, but the same process still applies if you use a rice cooker or a *donabe* (a Japanese clay cooking pot).

1. Measure the amount of rice you want to cook and rinse it in cold water for about 10 seconds. Then quickly drain the rice and place into a bowl.

2. Wash the rice a couple of times by stirring it in a circular motion with a so-called cat's paw (see next page) until the water becomes more translucent. This step will allow you to remove any excess starch and get rid of any impurities that originated from the harvesting process.

3. Drain the rice thoroughly so you can get a precise measurement of the amount of water needed in the next step.

4. Place the rice in a saucepan. Add the appropriate amount of cold water (filtered, if possible): just 1¼ cups plus a splash of water for every cup of rice.

5. Let the rice soak for at least 30 minutes in the cold water. If you cannot use water that is sufficiently purified, add a stick of *binchōtan* (see page 10) to the pot. While soaking, the rice will absorb the water, which will allow it to cook faster and will result in a softer texture (or a *fuwa fuwa* texture, as they say in Japanese).

6. After the rice is done soaking, place the saucepan over high heat, cover, and bring to a boil. Avoid lifting the lid off the saucepan while the rice is cooking.

7. Once boiling, reduce the heat to low and simmer until the rice has completely absorbed the water.

8. The lack of steam and a small "pshhhhht" sound will indicate that the rice is done cooking, generally after around 25–30 minutes. Remove the pot from the heat, and let the rice stand for about 10 minutes or until any remaining water is absorbed.

9. Gently mix the rice by "cutting" it with a flat instrument to let it oxygenate, and remove the charcoal. This helps the rice to reach a better density level. Put the lid back on to keep the rice from drying out.

Fun fact! **You can recycle the water you used to rinse your rice and use it as conditioner, as a drink in case of intestinal issues (if the rice is organic), as a weed killer, and even as a stain remover.**

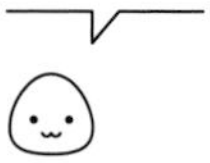

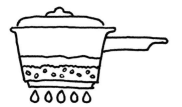

Shaping the Onigiri

Assemble the rice, water, salt, garnish, and *nori* sheet on your kitchen counter.

① Lightly wet the palms of your hands (repeat this step for every onigiri).

The *nori* sheet must be wrapped the correct way. The smooth, silky side should be on the inside, and the rough side should be on the outside.

② Spread 2–3 pinches of salt on the palms of your hands. Quick tip: use less salt if you're planning on serving and eating the onigiri immediately. If the garnish you prepared is only slightly salted, such as with tuna-mayo onigiri, then use three pinches of salt.

③ Take a portion of rice in one palm and form a small well.

④ Fill the hole with 1 tablespoon of garnish and cover with a smaller portion of rice.

⑤ Create a rough ball, and then start shaping a triangle little by little by leaving one hand flat and forming a 90-degree angle with your other hand. Turn the onigiri over three times to properly shape all three sides. During this step, it's important to remember not to press too hard on the rice and to be consistent while using a light touch during the motions.

⑥ Try imagining the roof of a house when shaping your onigiri.

⑦ Place the *nori* sheet so that you can hold the onigiri without your fingers touching the rice. There are several ways to do this: you can choose to cover the onigiri entirely, or just with a strip of *nori*, or even wrap it as if it were a kimono.

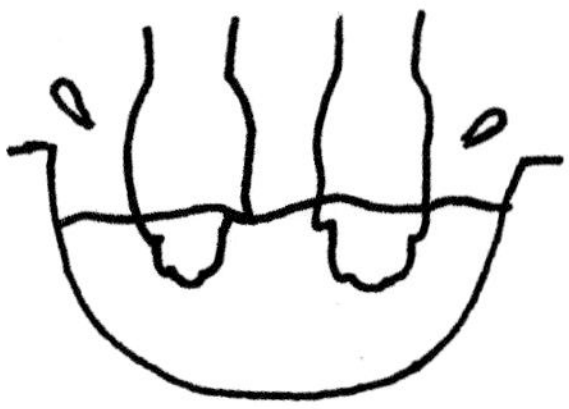

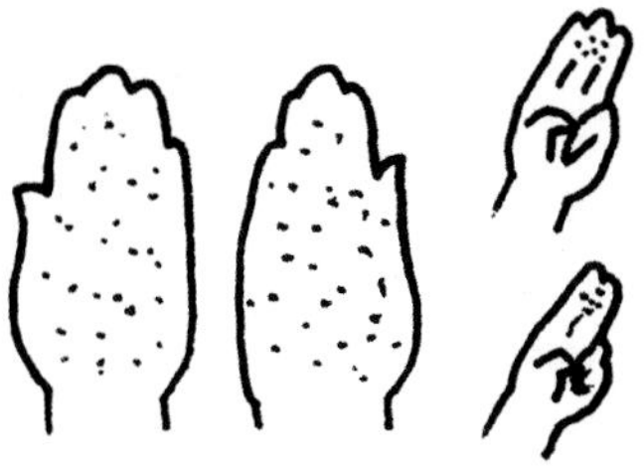

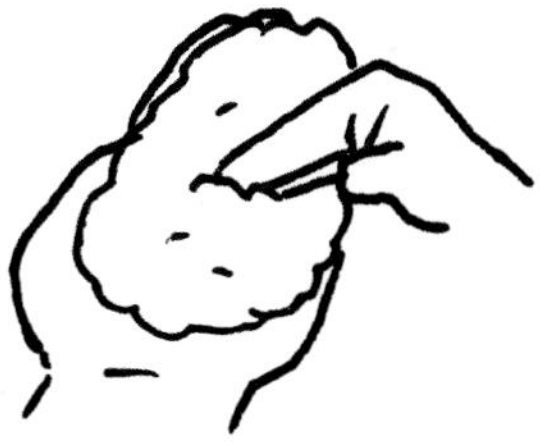

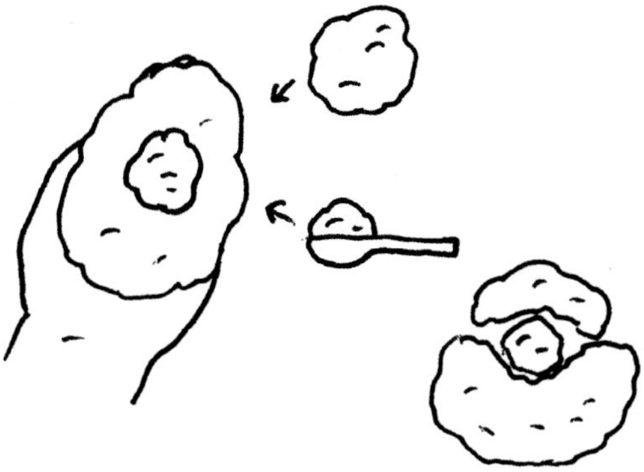

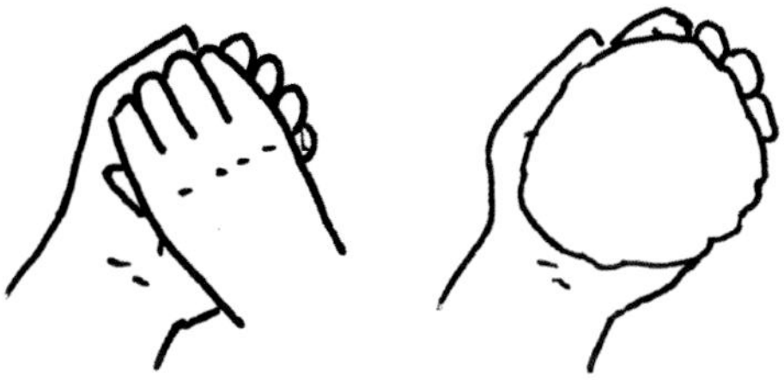

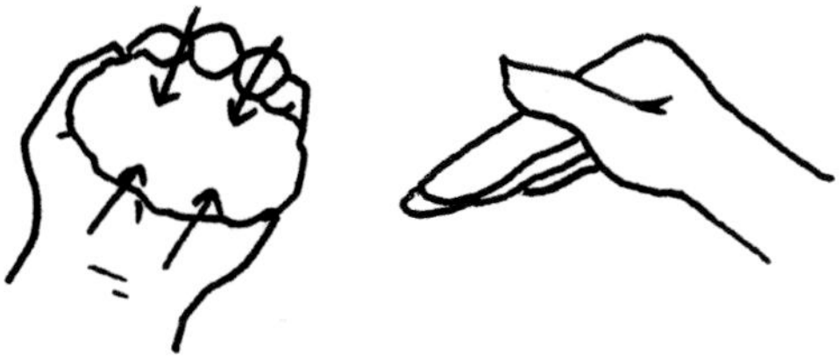

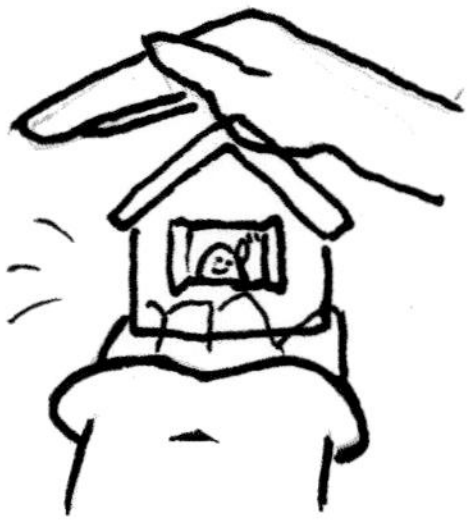

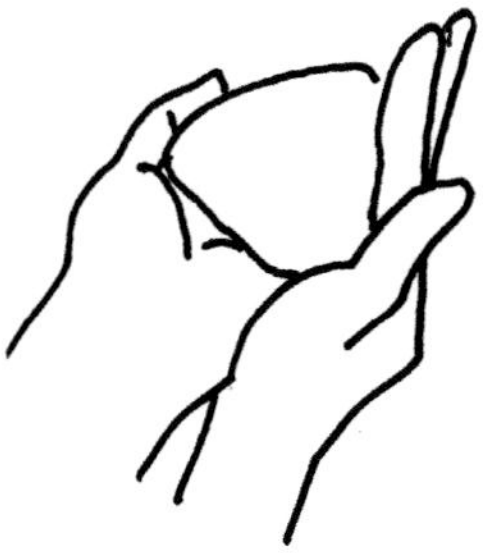

Storing and Wrapping

Onigiri taste the best they're made. If you want to store them for later, you can use plastic wrap or keep them in a hermetically sealed container.

Cooked rice will only last for a couple of days in the refrigerator in a closed container before expiring. If frozen, however, it can last for six to eight months. Onigiri go well with pickled foods (or *tsukemono*), miso soup, or even tea.

In Japan, onigiri wrapping has evolved since the mass commercialization of onigiri in the 1970s. Nowadays, we often find onigiri wrapped in a plastic wrapper that opens in three steps and includes a crunchy sheet of *nori*.

If you would prefer to avoid using plastic, then wrap and carry your onigiri using *furoshiki*, the Japanese art of wrapping.

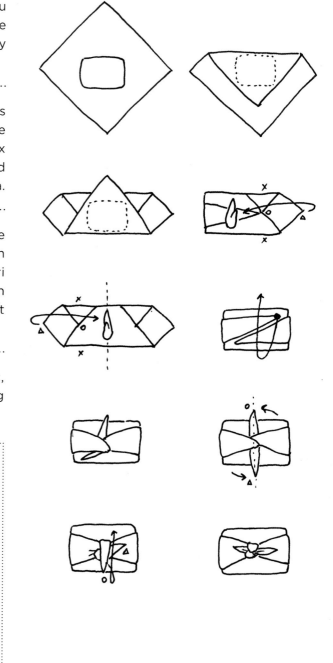

WHAT DOES *MOTTAINAI* MEAN?

Japanese people frequently use the word *mottainai*. The term itself expresses a feeling of regret toward throwing anything away that can still be used and a sense of pity toward unused leftovers. The term became globally well-known through the works of ecologist Wangarī Muta Maathai, who received the Nobel Peace Prize in 2004.

Now it's up to you! *Itadakimasu!*

Anecdotes

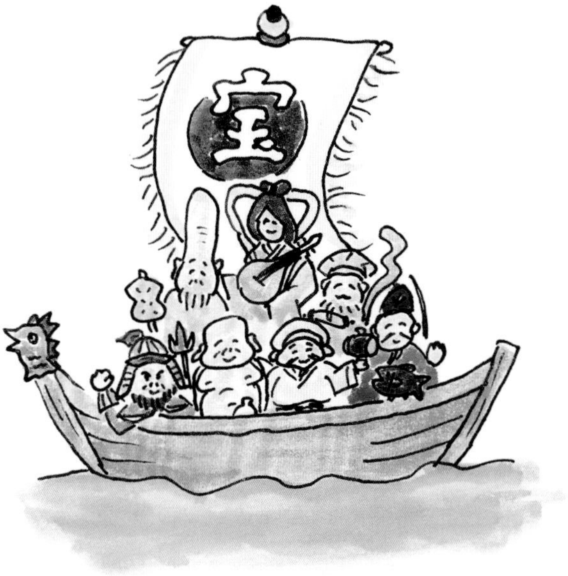
宝

SPIRITS RESIDE IN THE RICE

When Ai was small, her grandparents would often tell her that she had to finish her rice if she didn't want to be punished by the seven spirits that resided in the grains of rice. Why seven, you ask? Well, as it turns out, this number represents all the elements vital to creating rice: sun, water, earth, clouds, wind, insects, and humankind. This lesson has been passed down from one generation to the next to teach children to respect the effort put in by those who grow rice.

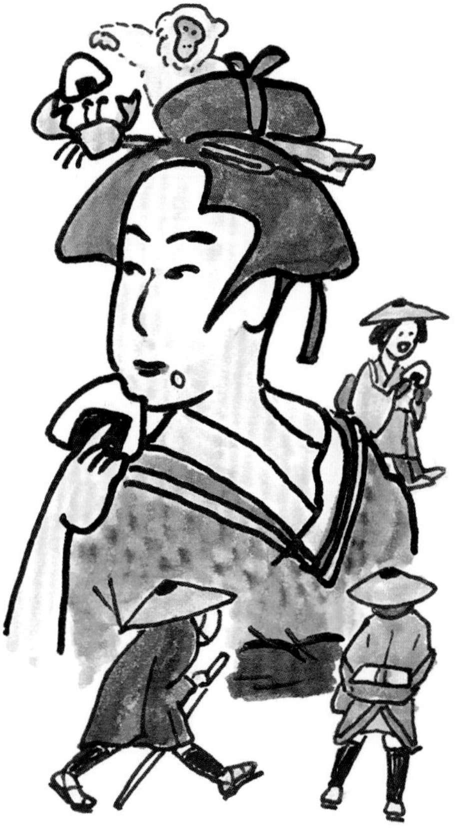

CHEW EACH BITE THIRTY TIMES

In Japan, we advocate chewing each bite thirty times before swallowing. Saliva helps break down the starch residing in sugars, so chewing for longer periods of time not only reduces the size of the actual food but, thanks to the saliva's help, also facilitates digestion. The starch contained in the rice is transformed into glucose, a carbohydrate that stimulates cerebral function. It's also a nutrient that is digested and then assimilated more slowly than wheat, making it more filling and allowing us to avoid experiencing glycemic peaks. So, concentrate on your chewing when you eat rice!

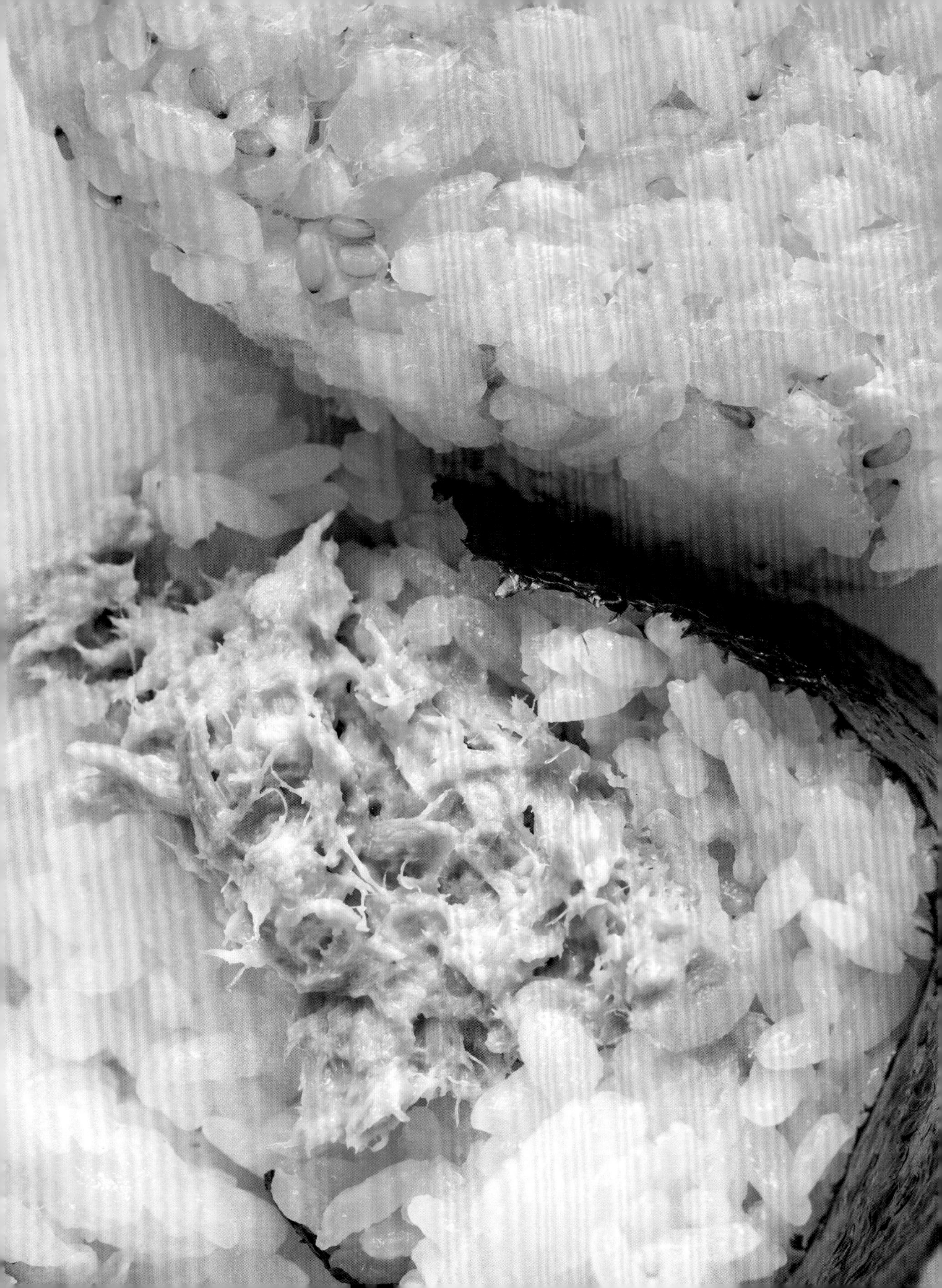

Fish

Mackerel with miso

🍙 × 6

1½ **cups rice**

7 **ounces mackerel,
    head and tail removed**

Hot water

7 **tablespoons water**

7 **tablespoons sake**

About 1 inch fresh ginger

2 **tablespoons miso**

2 **tablespoons mirin**

1 **tablespoon soy sauce**

2 **tablespoons
    granulated sugar**

To top it off

1 **tablespoon miso**

1 **tablespoon sake**

STEPS

Cook your rice (see page 12) and let it cool.

Slice your mackerel lengthwise into two pieces and then in half widthwise. Make an incision into the meat to allow for the sauce to be better absorbed.

Put the mackerel in a salad bowl. Fill the salad bowl with hot water (about 190°F/90°C) until the mackerel pieces are entirely submerged. After blanching the meat for about 2 minutes, rinse it under cold water.

Add the 7 tablespoons water and the 7 tablespoons of sake to a pan. Then peel and julienne the ginger, roughly ⅛ cup, before adding it to the mixture. Bring to a boil over medium heat. Add the mackerel to the boiling water with the skin side up, and skim the water thoroughly throughout.

Mix together 2 tablespoons of the miso, the *mirin*, the soy sauce, and the sugar in a small bowl. Take some of your mackerel broth and add it to the mixture. Once combined, gradually add the mixture back into the pan. Lower the heat and cover the pan with aluminum foil so the foil directly touches the mackerel (this is a drop lid, a Japanese simmering technique called *otoshi buta*), and let it simmer for about 13 minutes.

Remove the aluminum foil, and add the remaining 1 tablespoon of miso and the remaining 1 tablespoon of sake, repeating the process from the first half of the previous step. Let simmer for another 8–10 minutes or until the sauce thickens and turns a darker shade of brown.

Break up the meat into chunks, making sure to remove any bones. Add some sauce, and then garnish and shape your onigiri.

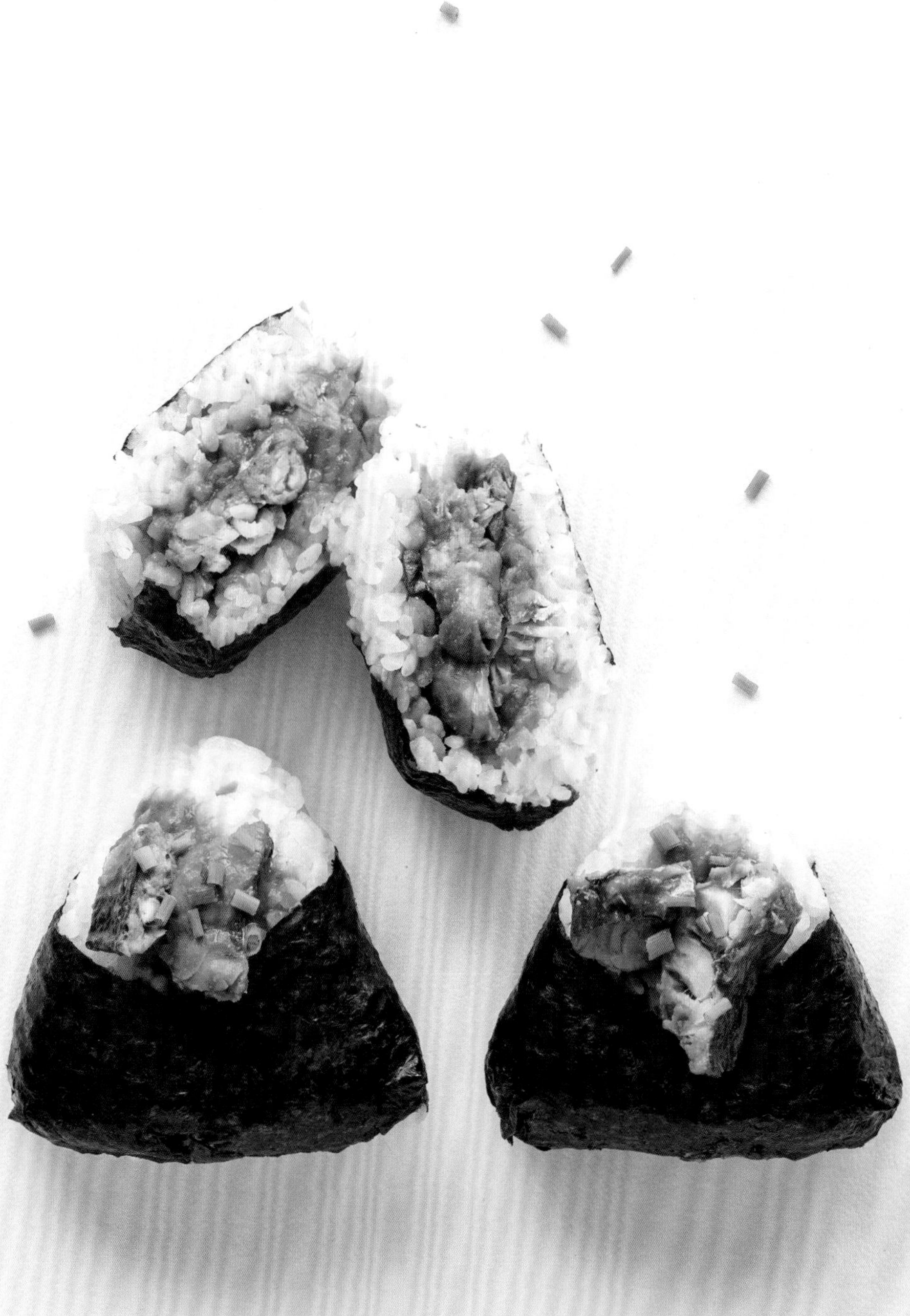

Cooking the mackerel with the bones left inside adds some depth to the sauce, but be sure to remove any remaining viscera. Also avoid letting the sauce form large bubbles, as this may cause the miso to lose its flavor.

Mackerel has a pronounced flavor, so poaching and rinsing it under cold water and then adding miso to it twice keeps the flavor in the onigiri, even when it isn't eaten immediately.

Chirashi

× 6

1½ **cups rice**

3–4 **large** *shiitake* **mushrooms**

1¾ **ounces carrots**

4 **tablespoons soy sauce**

4 **tablespoons** *mirin*

2 **tablespoons sugar**

¾ **cup plus 2 tablespoons water**

2 **ounces canned tuna in water, drained**

Around 15 pods edamame

Vinegar for sushi rice (if available, use about 10 percent of the total weight of the cooked rice)

4 **tablespoons rice vinegar**

STEPS

Cook your rice in a little under 1¼ cups water.

Cut the *shiitake* mushrooms into thin slices and your carrots into round slices, paysanne-style.

Heat the soy sauce, *mirin*, sugar, and water in a pan over medium heat. Bring to a boil, and then reduce heat to medium low. Add the *shiitake* mushrooms, carrots, and tuna. Put a sheet of aluminum foil that directly touches the mixture over the pan, and cook for 10 minutes.

Remove the foil and reduce heat to low, letting the mixture simmer for around 25 minutes until the liquid has completely evaporated.

Blanch the edamame for 1 minute, and then remove them from their pods and set them aside.

Move the cooked rice into a salad bowl. Pour the sushi rice vinegar over the rice, roughly 1 tablespoon at a time, and mix thoroughly. Use a folded or electric fan to aerate the rice.

Press down on the tuna mixture to remove any remaining liquid. Add the mixture to the dressed rice along with the edamame, and shape your onigiri.

Chirashi is a dish typically served at special events, such as traditional Japanese festivals or Hina Matsuri, the Japanese "Girls' Day." There are as many versions of chirashi as there are regions in Japan. It's often garnished with sashimi—however, as you might have noticed, this version doesn't include any. This family recipe was developed by my grandmother, who wanted to create a dish that my older sister, who doesn't like raw fish, could enjoy with all of us.

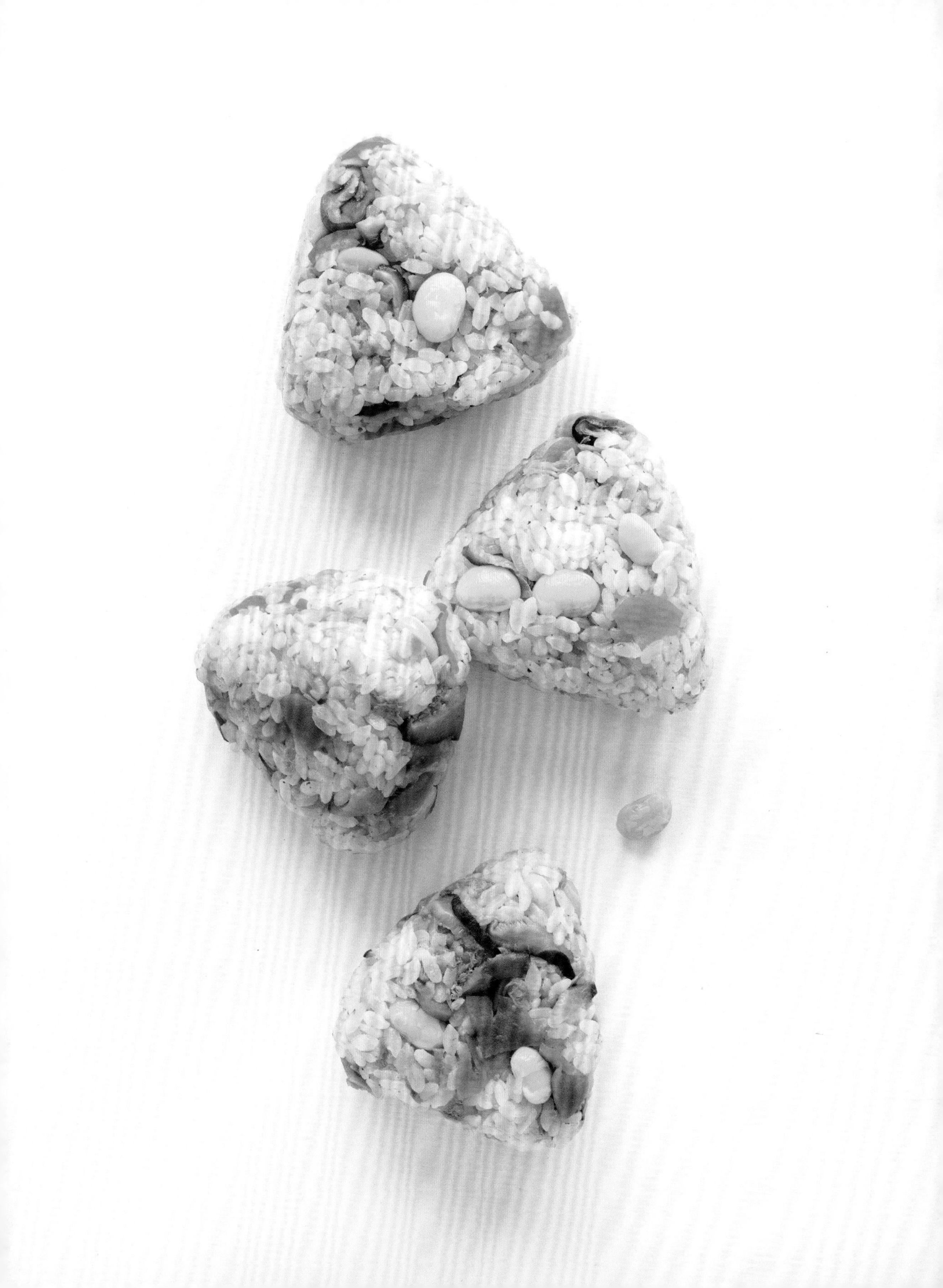

Tuna-mayo

 × 6

1½ cups rice

½ cup canned tuna in water

2 tablespoons mayonnaise

1 tablespoon soy sauce

Pepper, to taste

Japanese *ichimi* spice,
    to taste (optional)

STEPS

Cook your rice (see page 12) and let it cool.

Drain the canned tuna, pressing down on the tuna to remove as much liquid as possible.

Promptly mix the tuna-mayo in a bowl, and strain if later. Once you've created a smooth mixture, add the soy sauce and mix again until incorporated. Add pepper to taste and Japanese *ichimi* spice, if desired.

Add a heaping tablespoon of garnish in the middle of the onigiri, and then proceed to shaping.

This is one of the most basic onigiri recipes. Tuna-mayo onigiri have revolutionized the onigiri world. While today tuna-mayo is counted as the most popular garnish in Japan, for about 100 years before its creation, it was unfathomable for Japanese people to enjoy any garnishes outside *umeboshi* (Japanese plums) or *kombu* (Japanese kelp).

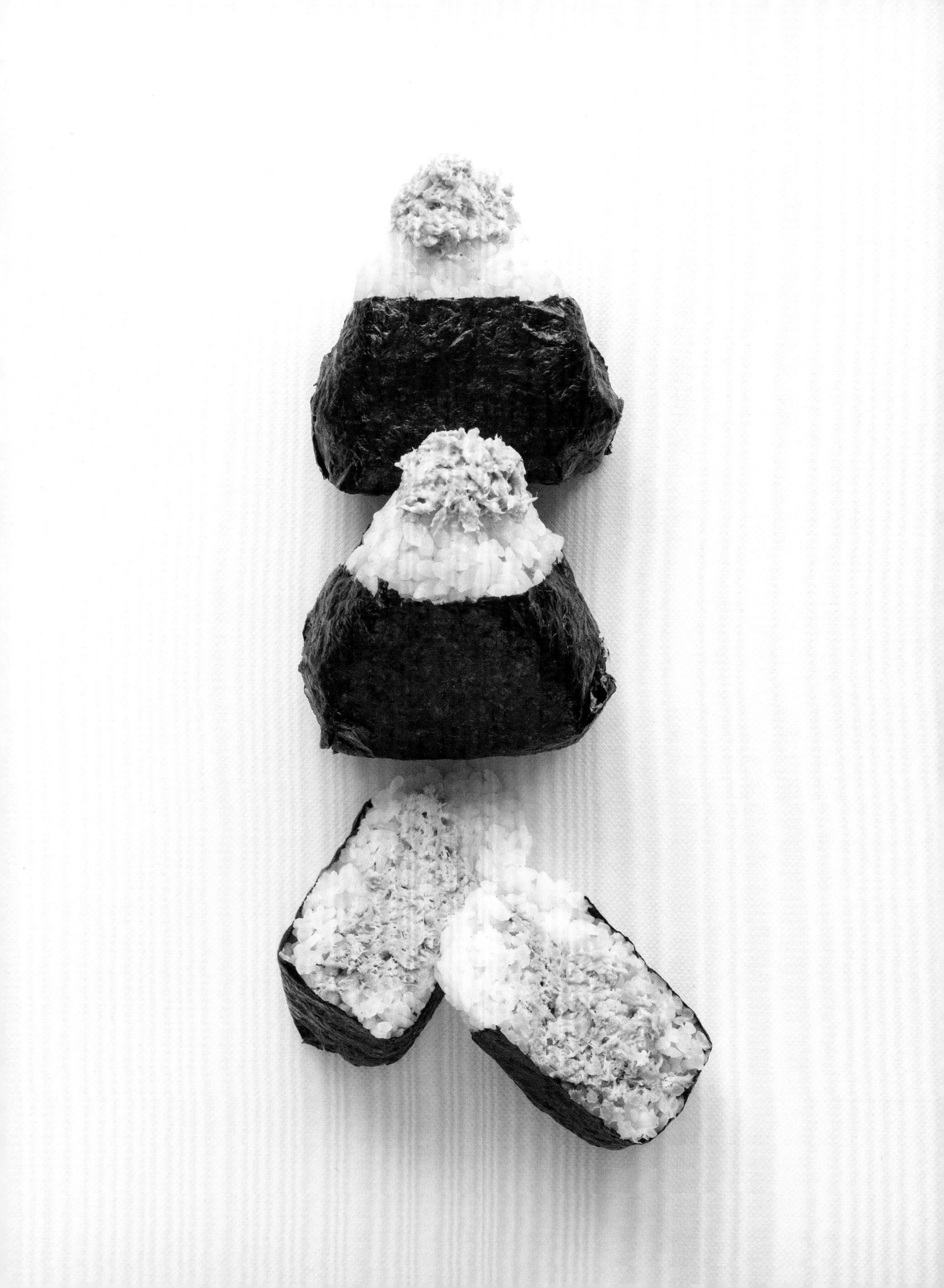

Salmon

🍙 × 6

1½ **cups rice**

2½ **ounces boneless, skinless salmon**

2 **tablespoons sake**

1 **tablespoon** *mirin*

Salt, to taste

1 **tablespoon toasted sesame oil**

1 **tablespoon toasted sesame seeds**

STEPS

Cook your rice (see page 12) and let it cool.

Place a pan over medium heat, then add the salmon. Pour the sake and *mirin* on top of the salmon.

After 4–6 minutes, break up the salmon in the pan before it finishes cooking. Add salt and let the salmon cook for an additional 3–4 minutes until all the liquid has finished evaporating.

Drizzle with sesame oil and immediately remove from heat.

Roughly mix the rice, salmon, and sesame seeds. Shape your onigiri.

If you substitute the sesame oil with another type of oil, you will end up with a completely different recipe. Olive oil, butter, coconut oil...the sky's the limit. Feel free to try out any combination that suits your fancy.

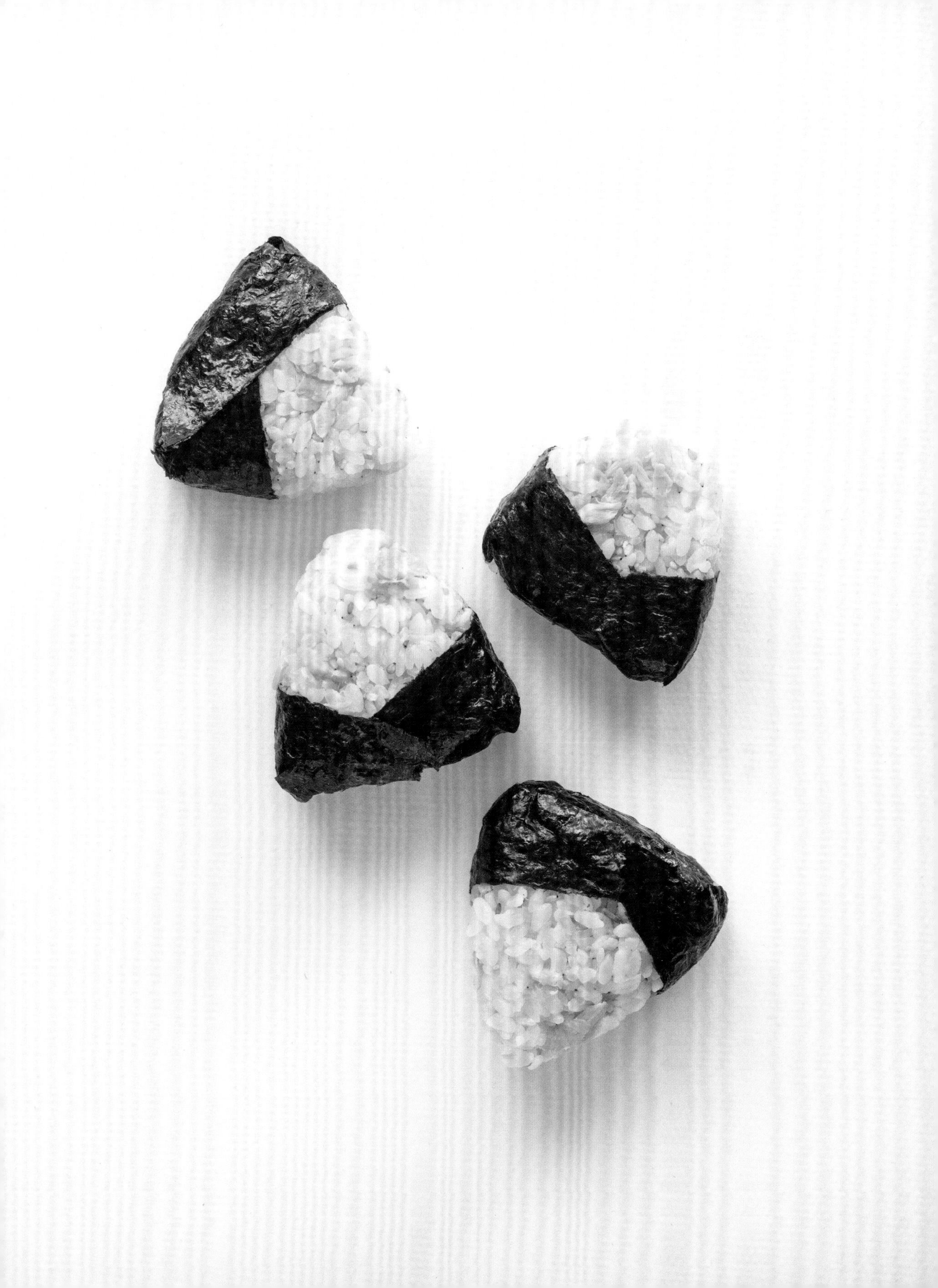

Russian-style onigiri

Chef Olivier Valade of the Château Saint-Jean in Montluçon, France

🍙 × 10

1½ **cups rice**

1¾ **ounces clotted cream**

⅓ **ounce shredded horseradish**

Salt and pepper, to taste

4 **eggs**

1 **white onion**

¼ **bunch curly parsley**

1¾ **ounces black caviar**

STEPS

Cook your rice (see page 12) and let it cool.

Mix the clotted cream with the horseradish, and then season with salt and pepper to taste. Store in a cool place.

Place the eggs in a medium pot over high heat. Bring the eggs to a boil and cook for 10 minutes. Remove the eggs from the pot and let them cool, or shock them in cold ice water for 10–15 minutes. Once you can safely touch the eggs, peel them and then separate the yolks from the whites. Pass the yolks, followed by the whites, through a sieve and finely mince.

Finely chop the onion and parsley leaves.

Prepare your onigiri and then, in layers, add to its center a dash of the horseradish cream, some egg mixture, some parsley, some onion, one heaping teaspoon of caviar, and another layer of horseradish cream to finish off.

Bon appétit!

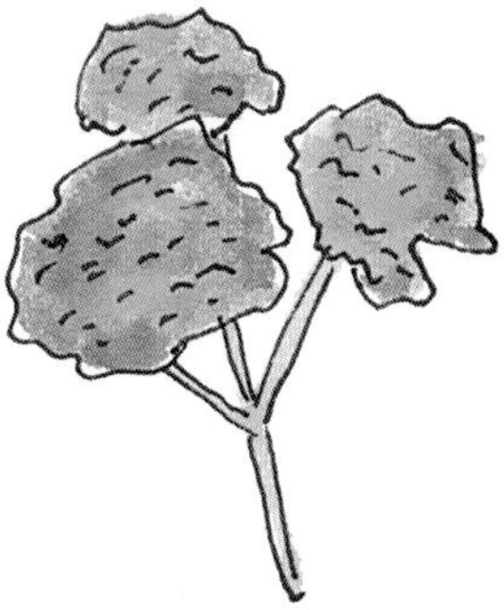
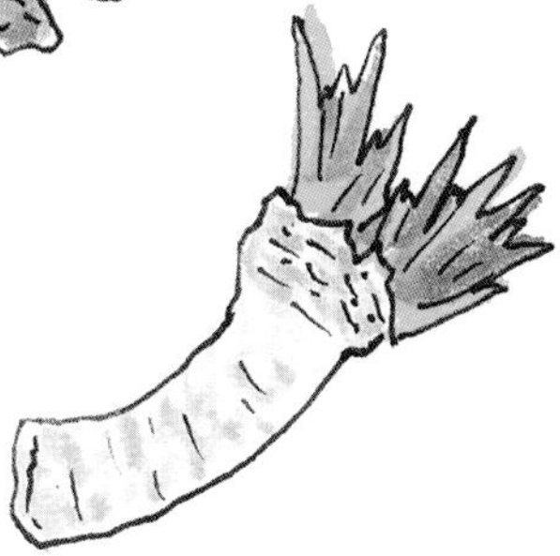
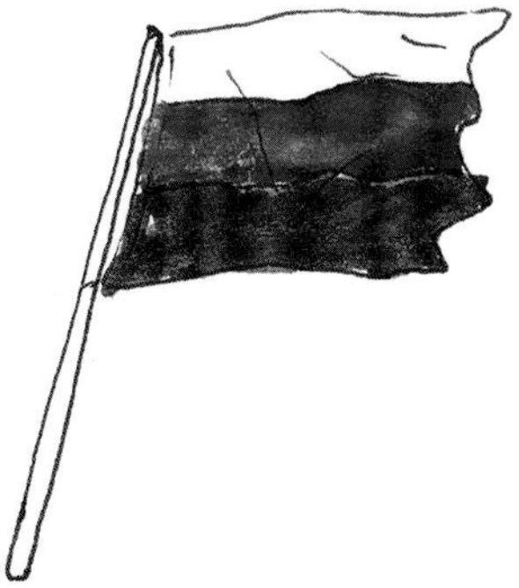
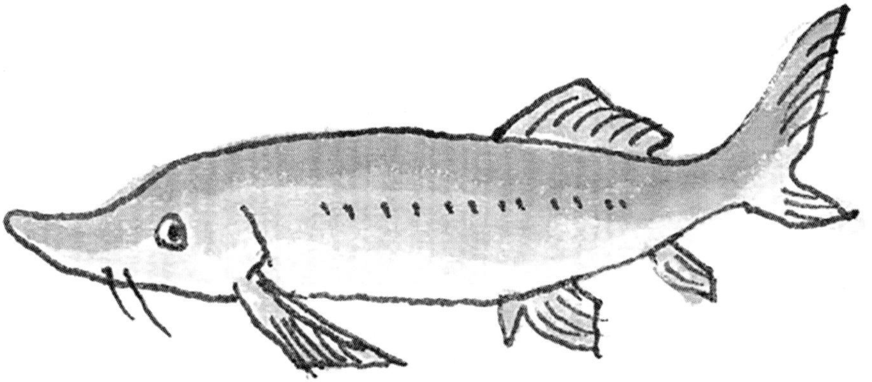
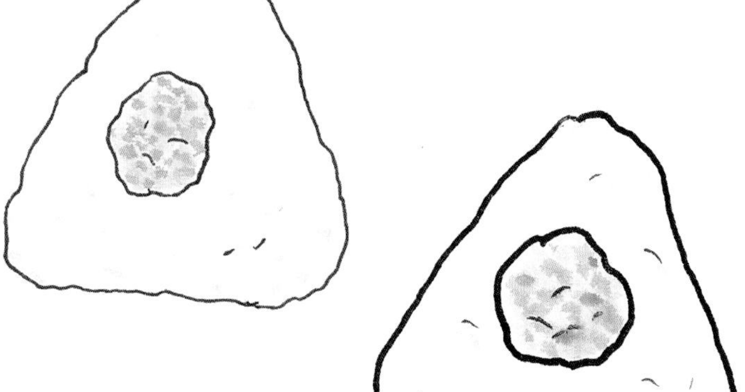

Okaka with wasabi

× 6

1½ cups rice

Up to 2 tablespoons wasabi, to taste

3 tablespoons soy sauce

2 cups dried bonito flakes, loosely packed

STEPS

Cook your rice (see page 12) and let it cool.

Dilute the wasabi in the soy sauce by combining in a bowl and mixing together. Add the dried bonito flakes, also known as *katsuobushi*, and mix.

Put the rice in a bowl and combine with the soy sauce mixture. To ensure you experience all of the different flavors when eating your onigiri, be careful not to mix to the point of it becoming one homogeneous mass. Shape your onigiri.

Despite the simplicity of this recipe the zing the wasabi brings combined with the umami of the dried bonito flakes will transform your onigiri into an irresistible snack. You can also top it with your favorite cheese. This is the recipe that my mother made for me around the age I was first able to eat wasabi. So to me, these onigiri are a symbol of maturity.

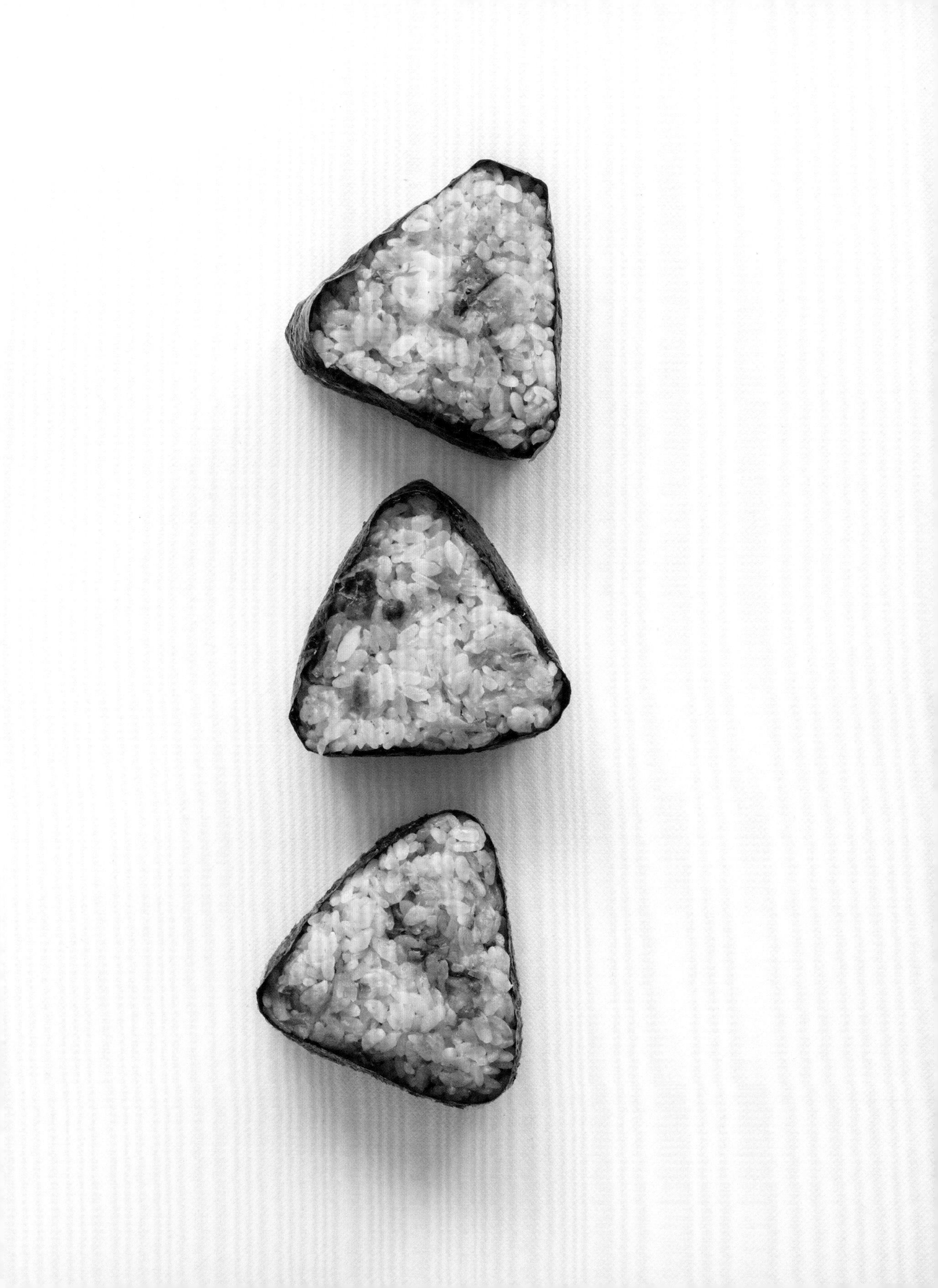

Scallops with miso

🍙 × 6

1½ cups rice

1 tablespoon butter

3 large scallops, quartered

2 tablespoons sake

1 tablespoon rice miso

1 tablespoon *mirin*

Pinch of black pepper

***Aonori* dried green laver flakes, to taste**

STEPS

Cook your rice (see page 12) and let it cool.

Place a pan over medium heat and add the butter. Before the butter melts, add the scallops and pour in the sake. Let the scallops cook while regularly flipping them until you start to see a change in color.

Mix the miso and *mirin* in a small bowl and add to the pan. Remove from heat once the scallops have been thoroughly coated by the sauce. Sprinkle with pepper and the *aonori* dried green laver flakes to taste.

Fill the center of your onigiri with the garnish doused in sauce and then shape.

A large variety of miso exists in Japan. In this case, I chose to go with a mildly flavored rice miso to better marry with the creaminess of the butter. That miso is made from soy, rice, and salt and is primarily found in the Japanese regions of Hokkaidō, Tōhoku, Kantō, and Kōshin'etsu.

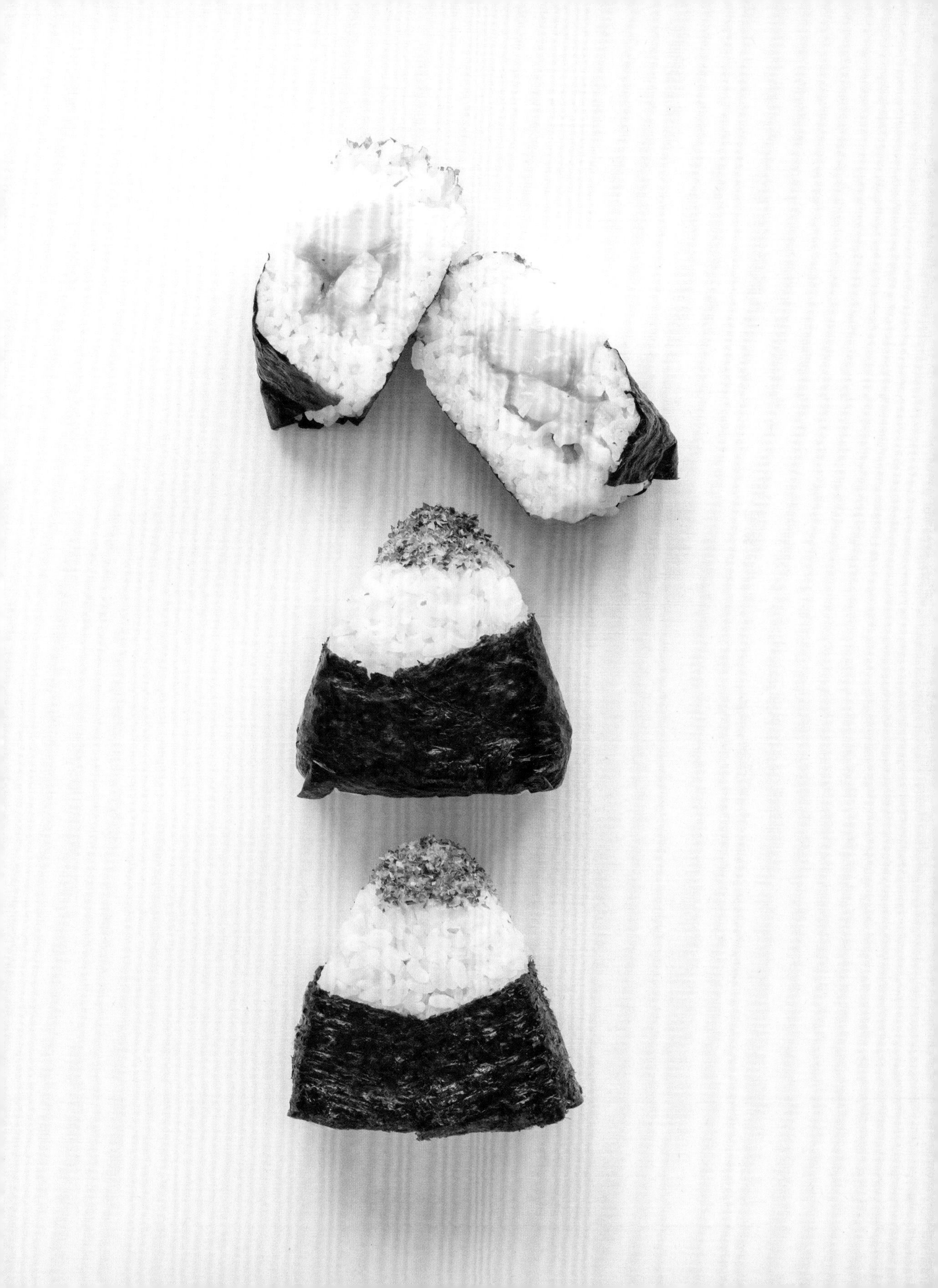

Ikura

⬢ × 6

1½ **cups rice**

3 — 4 **Japanese green**
***shiso* leaves**

1 **tablespoon sesame seeds**

1½ **teaspoons soy sauce**

1⅔ **ounces ikura**
(salmon roe)

Nori **seaweed, for assembly**

STEPS

Cook your rice (see page 12) and let it cool.

Remove the stems from the green *shiso* leaves. Layer the leaves on top of each other, roll them lengthwise, and then chop into thin pieces, also known as chiffonade. Mix the *shiso*, the sesame seeds, and the rice in a large bowl.

In a small bowl, pour the soy sauce on the salmon roe, also known as *ikura*, and stir carefully to keep the roe from bursting open.

Place a sheet of plastic wrap on a cutting board and put a handful of the rice in the shape of a triangle on the sheet. Without breaking the salmon roe open, spread a spoonful of roe in the middle of the rice, cover the roe with another handful of the rice, and then carefully bundle it together using the plastic wrap (avoid pressing on the onigiri!).

Leaving the onigiri on the cutting board, place both your hands on each side of it to form a triangle.

Place the onigiri in one hand, remove part of the plastic wrap, and cover with the *nori*. Roll the onigiri over in your hand, remove the remaining plastic wrap, and finish wrapping the onigiri with *nori*.

Salmon roe is a very delicate ingredient that easily breaks. If you press the onigiri with the usual force, the roe will burst open from the inside and become absorbed by the rice. Keep in mind that you should not press down on the onigiri during the shaping process. In Japan, salmon roe is marinated in soy sauce, but in France and the United States, the roe is sold in brine. Because of that, the salmon roe is already sufficiently salted, and you need only add a dash of soy sauce just before shaping your onigiri.

Prawn and avocado with wasabi

 × 6

1½ cups rice

Around 3 head-on prawns

Salt, for boiling

½ avocado

Dash of lemon juice

½ teaspoon wasabi

½ teaspoon soy sauce

1 tablespoon mayonnaise

STEPS

Cook your rice (see page 12) and let it cool.

Shell the prawns and remove the black line by slicing along the back and peeling it out. Then boil the shrimp in a pot in slightly salted water until the water turns pink.

Once boiled, drain the prawns and cut them into roughly ½-inch pieces. Cut the avocado into ½-inch pieces and combine with the prawns in a bowl. Sprinkle the mixture with the lemon juice.

Dilute the wasabi in the soy sauce by combining in a bowl and mixing together. Stir in the mayonnaise, and once combined, add to the prawn and avocado mixture.

Place the garnish in the center of your onigiri and then shape.

Be sure to thoroughly dilute the wasabi in your soy sauce so there aren't any wasabi lumps left. If you like the spicy taste and feeling of wasabi, you can add 1 teaspoon instead.

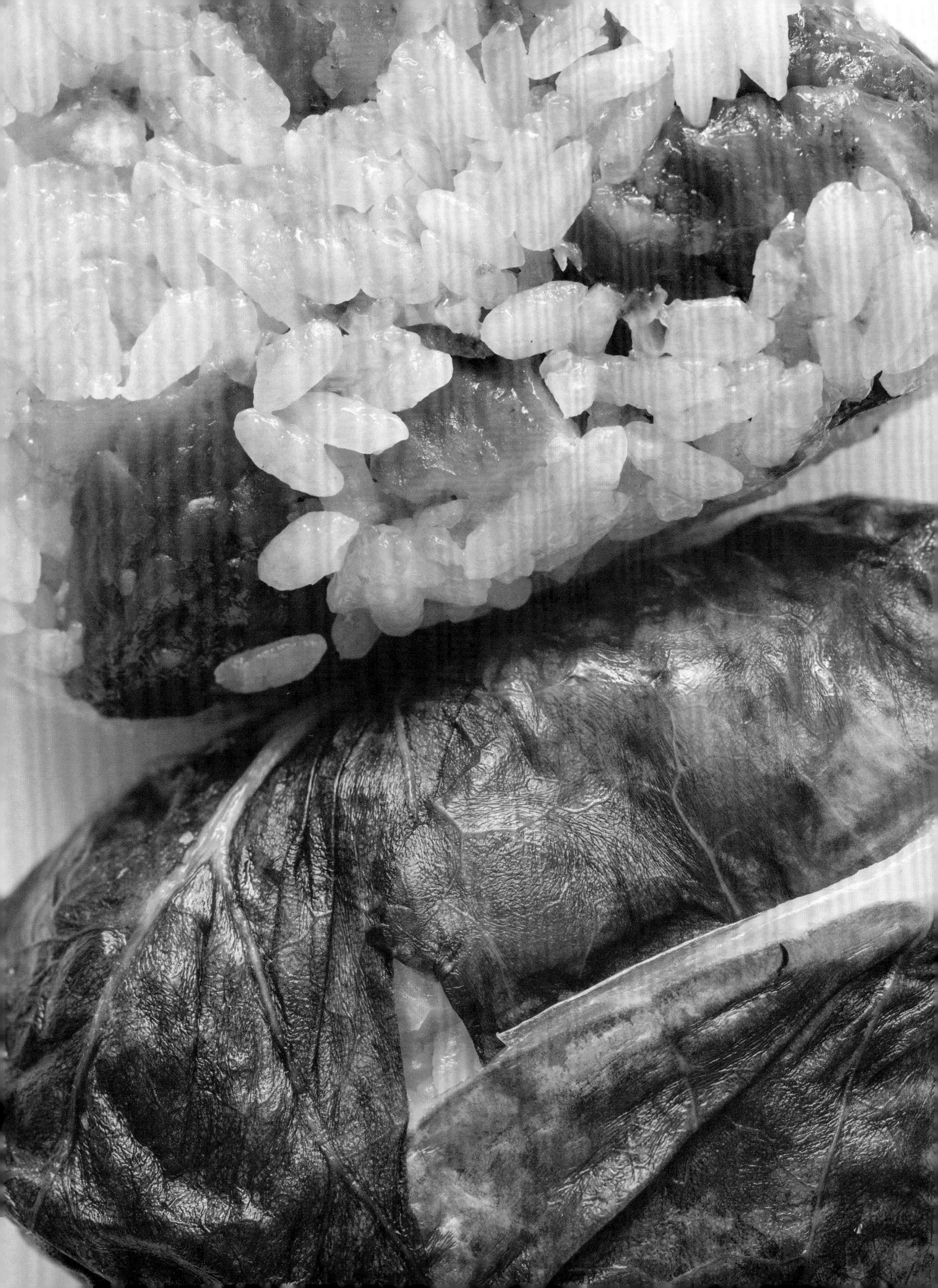

Veggies

Beet and kinpira

🍙 × 6

1½ cups rice

½ beetroot, julienned

1 tablespoon sesame oil

1 carrot, julienned

2 tablespoons soy sauce

1 tablespoon sake

1 tablespoon *mirin*

1 tablespoon sugar

1 tablespoon chili powder

1 tablespoon sesame seeds

STEPS

Cook your rice (see page 12) and let it cool.

Soak the beetroot in a small bowl of water for about 5 minutes, and then drain the beetroot slices.

Place a pan over medium heat and pour the sesame oil into the pan. Add the beetroot and carrot, and cook.

Once the vegetables are tender, add the soy sauce, sake, *mirin*, and sugar to the pan. Cook long enough to evaporate the alcohol and dissolve the sugar. Sprinkle with chili powder and immediately remove from the heat and drain.

Move the vegetables to a bowl and add the rice and then the sesame seeds. Shape your onigiri.

In Japan, *kinpira* is a dish that is usually made with burdock root, but if you can't find any, you can create a perfectly delicious version using Jerusalem artichokes or celeriac. For extra texture, I recommend adding some thinly sliced *konnyaku*, also known as yam cake.

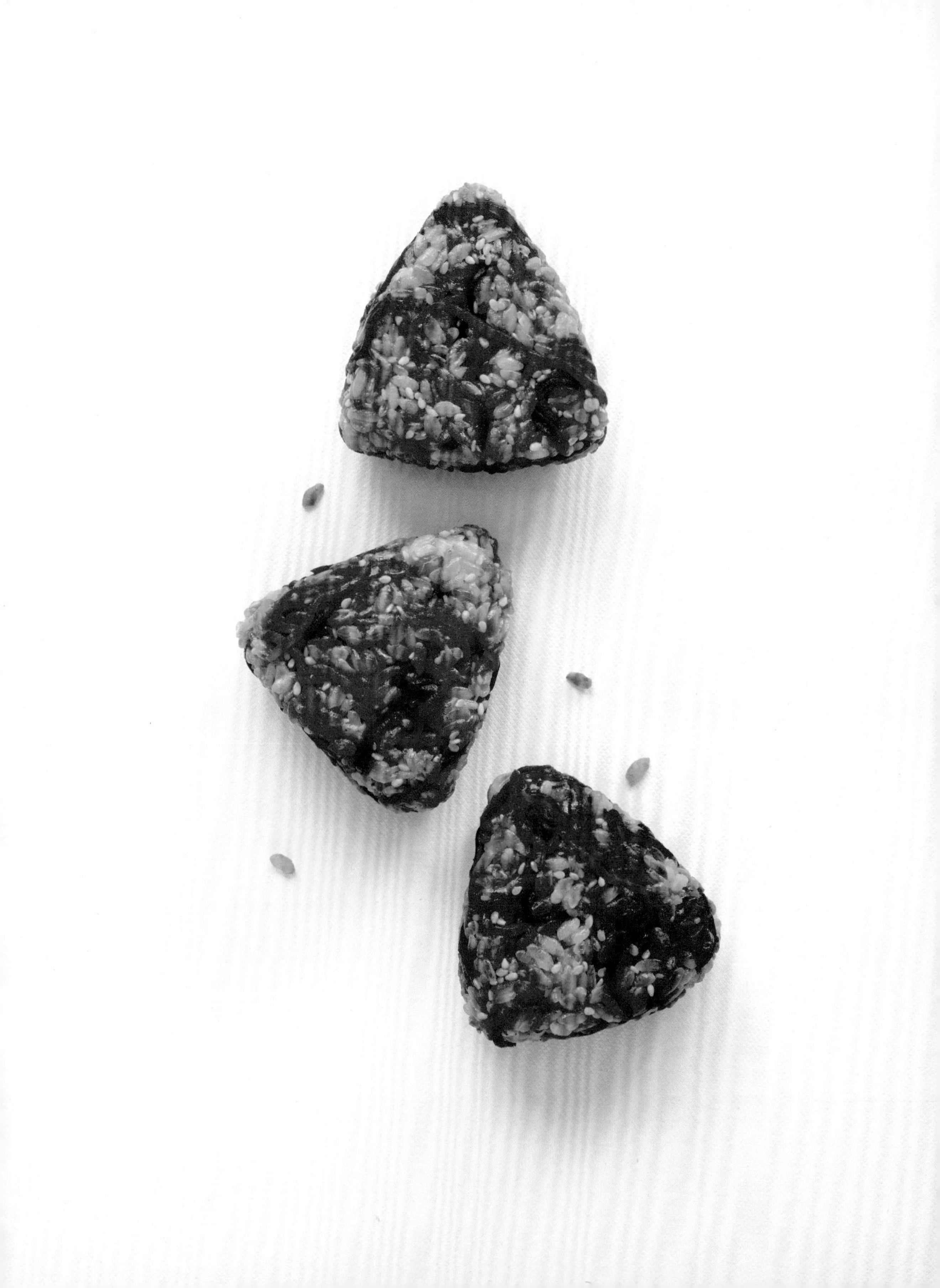

Yakimeshi

⬤ × 6

1½ cups rice

4 thin slices smoked bacon

1 tablespoon grilled sesame oil

2 eggs

1¾ ounces spring onion, chopped

1¾ ounces carrot, chopped

1 clove garlic, minced

1 tablespoon soy sauce

Salt and pepper, to taste

STEPS

Cook your rice (see page 12) and let it cool.

Sauté the bacon for 3–4 minutes until browned, then drain the fat.

Heat the sesame oil in a separate pan over medium-high heat. Beat the eggs, and then add them to the pan. Start whisking immediately.

Add the rice before the eggs are fully cooked. Stir well to keep the rice from clumping.

Add the onion, carrot, garlic, and smoked bacon. Once the garlic's aroma starts spreading, carefully add the soy sauce. Sprinkle with salt and pepper to taste. Shape your onigiri.

It's important to quickly sauté the yakimeshi. I would recommend using cool leftover rice because it will stick less and also help you use up rice that might otherwise go to waste. If the rice is a bit dry or oily, use plastic wrap when you shape the onigiri.

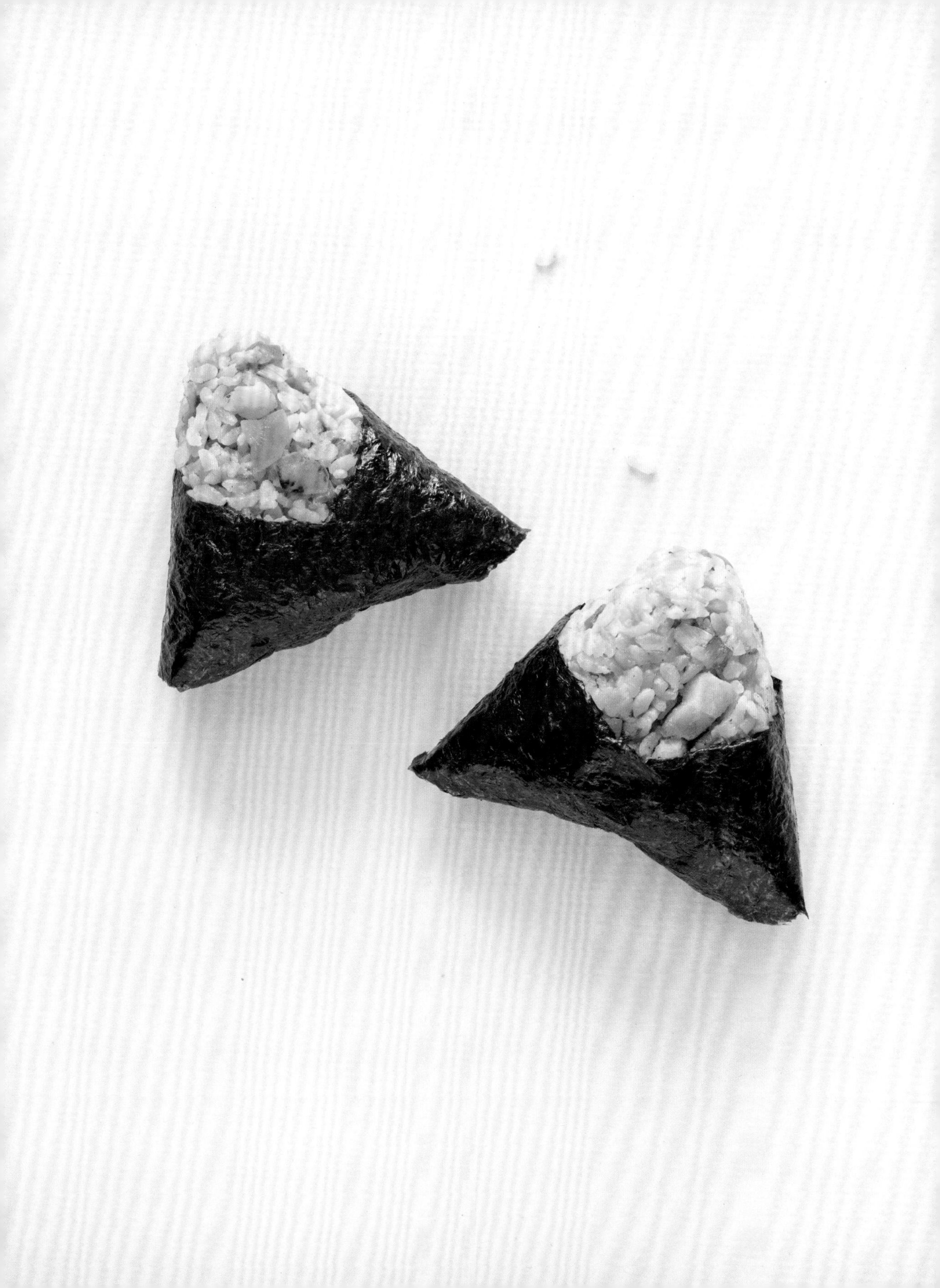

Fried soboro

Chef Noboru Mukaiyama of Nagoya,
Aichi Prefecture, Japan

🍙 × 6

1½ cups rice

1½ teaspoons sunflower oil
(or toasted sesame oil)

3 slices fried *abura-age*
tofu, degreased
and sliced*

¼ leek, sliced
(white part only)

Just under 7 tablespoons
dashi bouillon

1 tablespoon
powdered sugar

1 tablespoon dark
soy sauce

Pinch of powdered
aonori seaweed

STEPS

Cook your rice (see page 12) and let it cool.

Heat the sunflower oil in a pan. Sauté the tofu and leek in the pan for 3–4 minutes. Add the *dashi* bouillon, the powdered sugar, the soy sauce, and a pinch of *aonori*.

Place the garnish in the center of your onigiri and then shape.

Abura-age is made by frying thin slices of tofu. In addition to serving as a garnish for onigiri, it is added to miso soup and used to make inari sushi. It can even be grilled with some grated-ginger soy sauce. It's a highly versatile ingredient that can be used in a thousand ways.

Both vegetarians and vegans can use it to add protein to a dish. This recipe requires the abura-age to be degreased beforehand. To do this, place it on a fine sieve and pour a large quantity of boiling hot water over it. Then wipe off any excess with some paper towels.

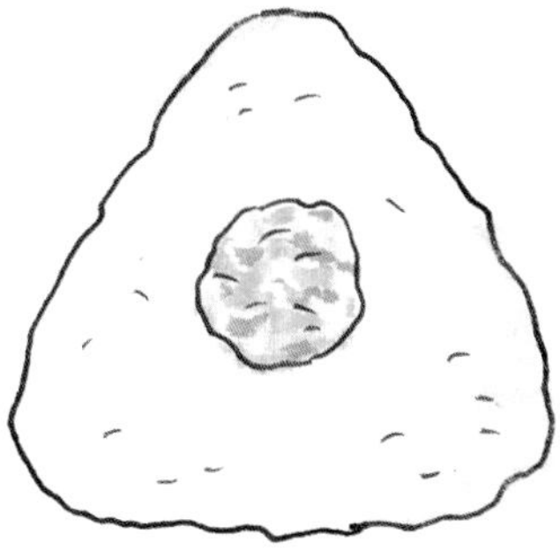

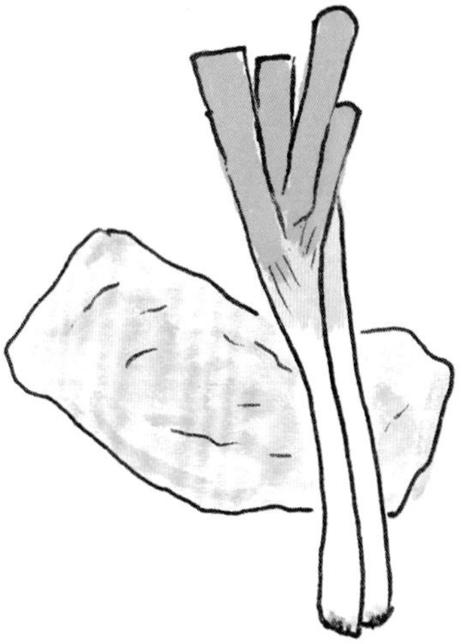

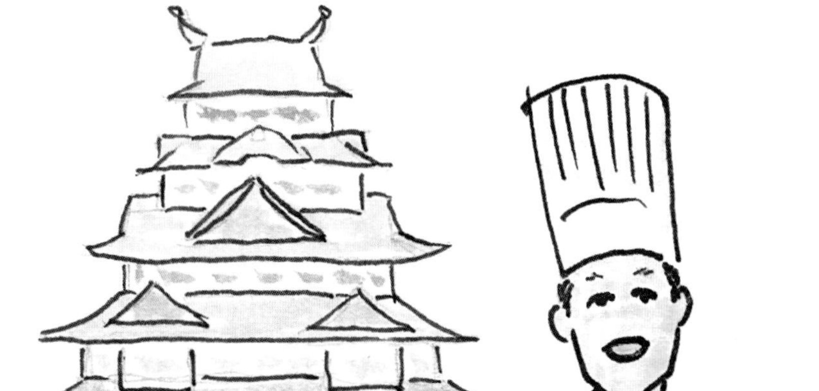

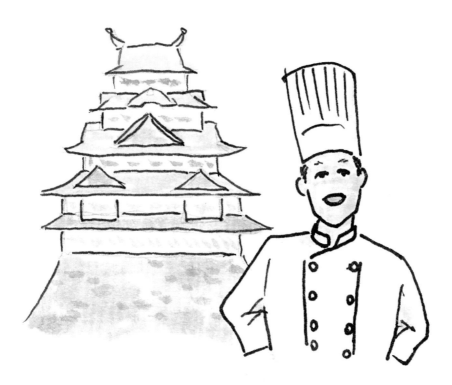

Chestnut

⬭ × 6

1 cup sticky or sweet glutinous rice

1 cup white rice

1½ cups water

1 pound roasted whole chestnuts, skin left on

¼ cup sake

1 teaspoon salt

STEPS

Wash both types of rice together and let them soak in about 1½ cups of water.

Soak the chestnuts in hot water for about 30 minutes so the skin and peel become soft. If chestnuts are out of season, roasted whole chestnuts and chestnuts in simple syrup should still be available.

Peel the chestnuts. If you are having difficulty doing this by hand, cut off the base of the chestnuts with a sturdy knife. Repeat this step for the second layer of skin. Once all the chestnuts have been peeled, let them soak in water for another 10 minutes. If using already processed chestnuts, skip the peeling and initial soaking stage. Soak the processed chestnuts for 10 minutes.

Pour the sake and salt onto the rice. Briefly stir, then add the chestnuts and let the whole mixture rest in the bowl until the chestnuts have turned soft.

Once done cooking, use a rice paddle to gently mix while crushing the chestnuts. Shape your onigiri.

When eating *okowa* (the name of this type of rice blend) on its own, it's better to leave the chestnuts whole to give the dish some character. But if the chestnuts are left whole when used to garnish onigiri, they could end up falling out. By slightly crushing them and mixing them into the rice, they spread evenly throughout the onigiri, which makes for a more pleasant eating experience.

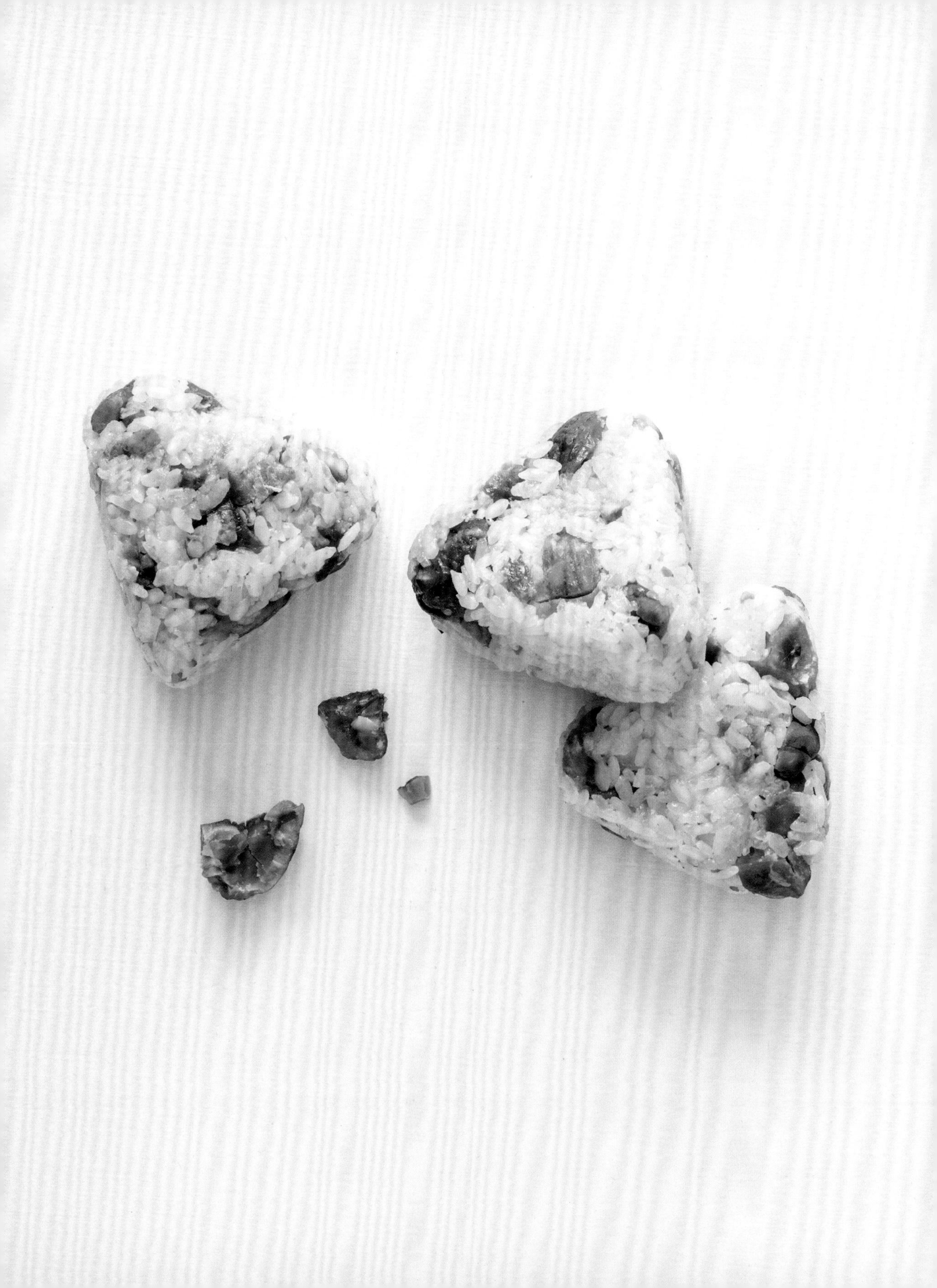

Kombu

⊙ × 6

1 tablespoon black rice

1 tablespoon red rice

3½ ounces *kombu* kelp

3 tablespoons soy sauce

1 tablespoon rice vinegar

2 teaspoons sake

2 teaspoons *mirin*

2 teaspoons sugar

STEPS

Wash both types of rice together. Let the rice soak for 30 minutes before cooking the rice as usual.

Cut the *kombu* into pieces roughly ¾ inch thick (try to use the thicker middle parts, and cut with scissors if necessary).

Place the *kombu*, soy sauce, rice vinegar, sake, *mirin*, and sugar in a frying pan over medium heat. Once boiling, lower the heat and let simmer for 15–20 minutes, or until tender and easily chewed.

As soon as your sauce has been reduced, remove from heat and let it cool. Drain the *kombu*.

Once the rice is done cooking, gently mix in the sauce.

Place the *kombu* in the middle of your onigiri and shape.

Unlike white rice, black and red rices are full of vitamins, minerals, proteins, and anthocyanins, which are great for your health. The grains hold up better when cooked and require slightly more chewing—the added texture creates an experience different from regular white rice. In Japan, this type of rice blend is popular with young women and people concerned about their health. White rice pairs very well with cereals and seeds such as quinoa, sesame seeds, whole-grain rice, barley, and even pumpkin seeds.

Goma edamame

🍙 × 6

1½ cups rice

1 cup edamame

2 tablespoons toasted sesame seeds

1 tablespoon grilled sesame oil

1 teaspoon salt

Pinch of pepper

STEPS

Cook your rice (see page 12) and let it cool.

Blanch the edamame for 2–5 minutes, until they have turned a brighter green, and then peel. Transfer the beans to a bowl.

Mix the sesame seeds, sesame oil, salt, and pepper in a bowl. Once combined, pour over the edamame.

Add the rice and stir until combined. Shape your onigiri.

The sesame oil may cause the edamame to fall out when you're shaping the onigiri. Try to wrap the edamame with the rice as much as possible during the shaping process. If the edamame still keep slipping out, use plastic wrap to shape the onigiri.

Tofu curry

⬤ × 6

1½ cups rice

About 4 pieces of dried tomatoes

2 tablespoons plus 1½ teaspoons hot water

Around 1 small carrot

2 spring onions

¼ block firm tofu

Oil, for cooking (neutral in flavor)

1 tablespoon curry powder

1 tablespoon sugar

1 tablespoon soy sauce

1 tablespoon tomato paste

STEPS

Cook your rice (see page 12) and let it cool.

Rehydrate the dried tomatoes in hot water for about five minutes or until softened, then drain them. Set aside the water.

Dice the carrot and onions.

Drain and dry the tofu with paper towels or cloth, and then tear the tofu into small pieces by hand.

Heat the oil of your choice in a frying pan over medium heat. Add the tofu and sauté. Reduce to low-medium heat, add the dried tomatoes, carrots, and spring onions to the pan, and sauté for about 4–5 minutes, until tender. Add the curry powder, the sugar, the soy sauce, the tomato paste, and the water you soaked the dried tomatoes in, and let simmer while stirring. Once the sauce has reduced and thickened, remove from heat.

Gently mix the garnish and rice in a large bowl. Shape your onigiri.

If you are using firm tofu, be sure to strain it. Otherwise, go for the extra-firm variety. The salt level of curry powders you can find in supermarkets differs depending on the brand, so be sure to adjust the amount of soy sauce you use by tasting as you go. (In my recipes, I use spices that do not contain any salt.)

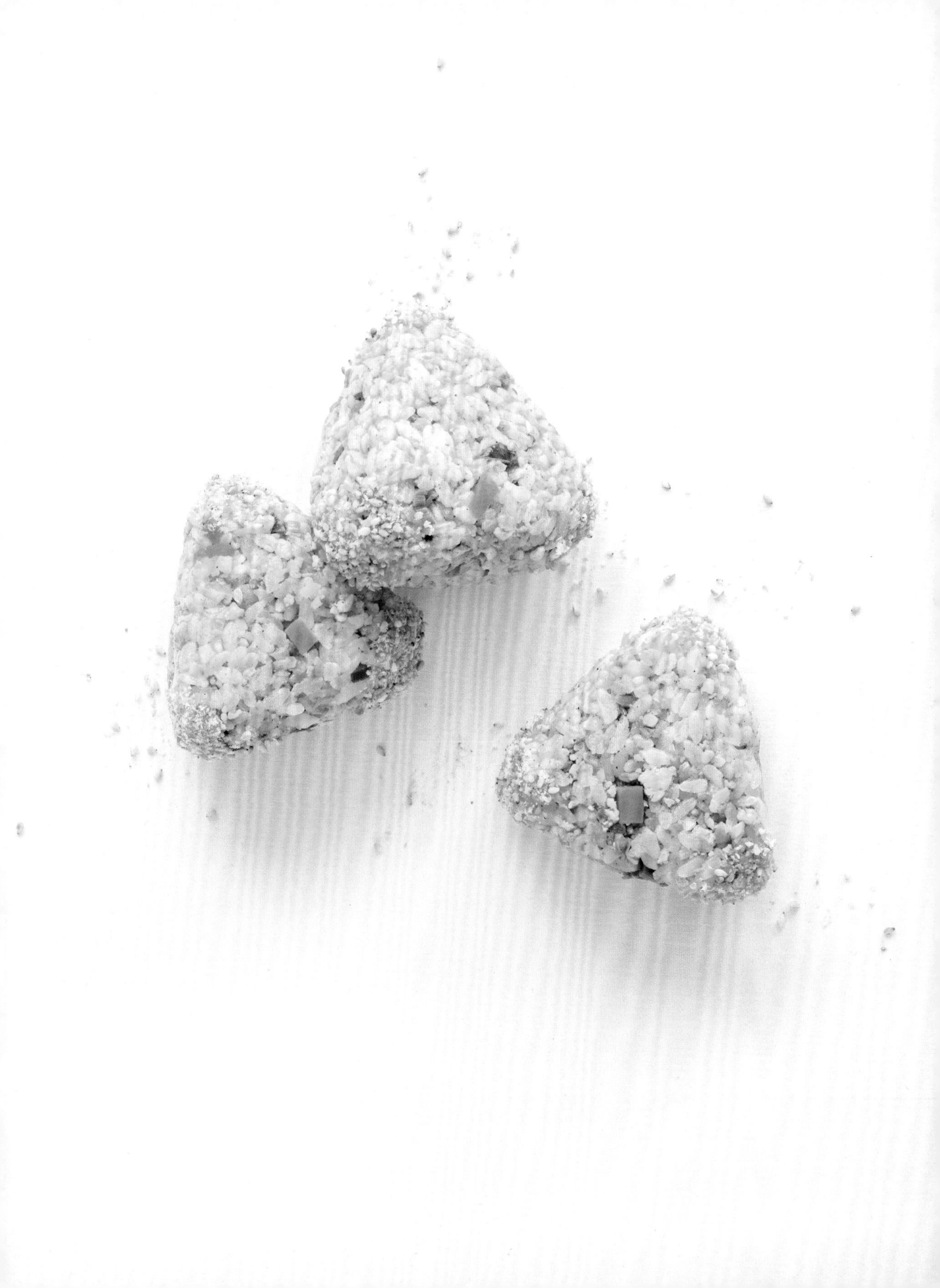

Shiitake

🍙 × 6

6 dried *shiitake* mushrooms

**1¼ cups *shiitake*
soaking water**

1½ cups rice

3 tablespoons soy sauce

3 tablespoons *mirin*

**2 tablespoons
granulated sugar**

STEPS

Soak the *shiitake* mushrooms in water and place in the refrigerator a day beforehand. After soaking, set aside the water and remove the *shiitake* stems. Slice the caps into thin strips.

Cook your rice (see page 12) and let it cool.

Place the soaking water, soy sauce, *mirin*, sugar, and *shiitake* mushrooms into a pan, and bring to a boil over medium heat. Reduce heat to low, cover the pan with a sheet of aluminum foil or a lid, and let simmer for 15 minutes.

Remove the aluminum foil or lid and continue to cook the mixture for around 10 minutes, until the sauce is reduced. Remove from heat and let cool (this step is very important to lock in the flavors).

Slightly strain the garnish but do not squeeze it, and then place in the center of your onigiri before shaping (be careful not to leave too much sauce or your onigiri will not hold their shape).

If you use fresh *shiitake* instead of dried, you'll bring out the umami, and the texture will be even creamier in your mouth. Whether they're fresh or dry, it's worth leaving the mushrooms out in the sun, gills up, for about 2 hours before cooking. Doing this will allow them to increase their level of vitamin D_2. It is also extremely important to soak them before use. If they're too hard, they could bring a dash of bitterness to your dish.

Sweet potato

⬤ × 6

1½ cups rice

5¼ ounces white sweet potatoes, peeled and cubed

1 tablespoon sake

1 teaspoon salt

¾ ounces (20 grams or about 1½ tablespoons) butter

2 tablespoons black sesame seeds

STEPS

Wash your rice and let it soak in 1 1/2 cups water for about 30 minutes.

Soak the sweet potato cubes in water for about 5 minutes, then drain.

Pour the sake and salt on the rice and mix briefly. Add the sweet potatoes to the top of the mixture, and cook until the sweet potatoes are fork tender.

Once the rice has finished cooking, wait 10 minutes, then mix in the butter and sesame seeds. Shape your onigiri.

Use the white-flesh variety of sweet potatoes. If you use purple sweet potatoes, the dish will turn out a lot sweeter. If you choose the more common orange variety, however, you'll need to substitute the sake for some *mirin* to get a more well-rounded flavor.

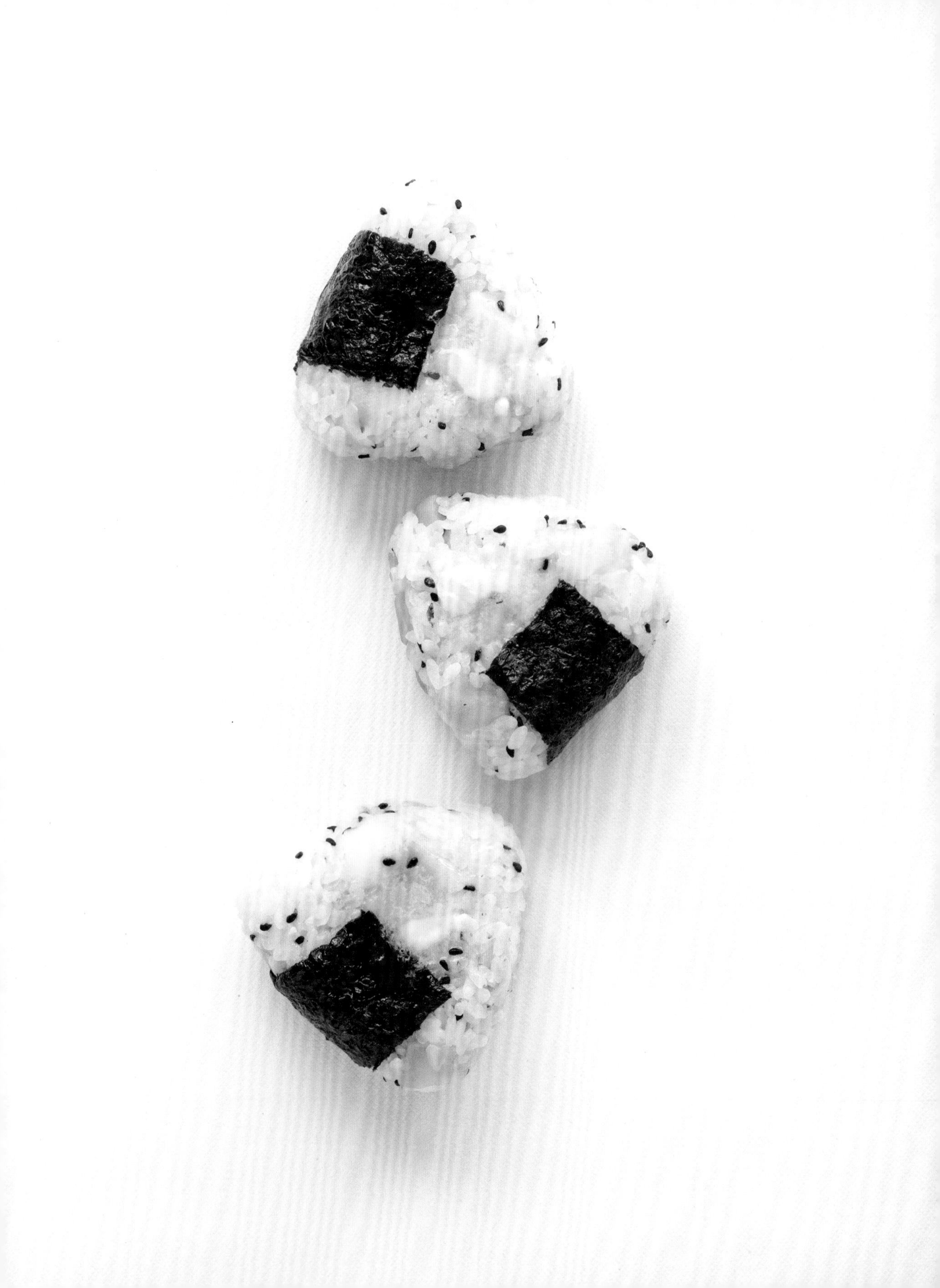

Nut and miso

🍙 × 6

STEPS

1½ **cups rice**

3½ **ounces nuts,**
roughly chopped

2 **tablespoons** *mirin*

2 **tablespoons red miso**

1½ **tablespoons**
granulated sugar

2 **teaspoons creamy**
peanut butter

Cook your rice (see page 12) and let it cool.

Brown the nuts in a frying pan over medium heat, stirring frequently so the nuts do not get overly toasted and hard. Wait about 3 minutes for the nuts to release their aroma. Taste a piece to make sure it cracks as you bite into it.

Add the *mirin* and bring the mixture to a boil. Reduce heat to low, and mix in the miso and sugar. Once the mixture is hot, gradually stir in the peanut butter. Once combined, immediately remove from heat (don't let it boil!).

Place the garnish in the middle of the rice and shape your onigiri.

This nut miso tastes very good when you coat the exterior of the onigiri with it and grill it. Red miso has a longer fermentation period, providing a richer and more intense taste. You can also take it one step further by adding cubed or melted brie to the mix.

Mehari

⬤ × 6

STEPS

1½ **cups rice**

4–6 leaves Swiss chard

½ **teaspoon salt**

1 tablespoon soy sauce

1 tablespoon *mirin*

Cook your rice (see page 12) and let it cool.

Separate the Swiss chard leaves from the stems, retaining both parts. Slice the stems into pieces roughly ¼ inch wide.

Place the stem pieces with the salt in a plastic freezer bag and massage. Close the bag and put it in the refrigerator.

In a pot, bring a large quantity of water to a boil. Add the chard leaves, and blanch for about 1 minute. Drain the leaves and then immediately rinse with ice-cold water.

Press the leaves with a paper towel to drain them of any excess water. Transfer to a bowl and add the soy sauce and *mirin*. Let the leaves marinate in the mixture.

Remove the chard stems from the and mix with the rice in a bowl. Shape your onigiri and wrap them in the chard leaves after lightly wringing them out.

If you are using chard of different color varieties, be sure to salt them separately to avoid mixing the colors.

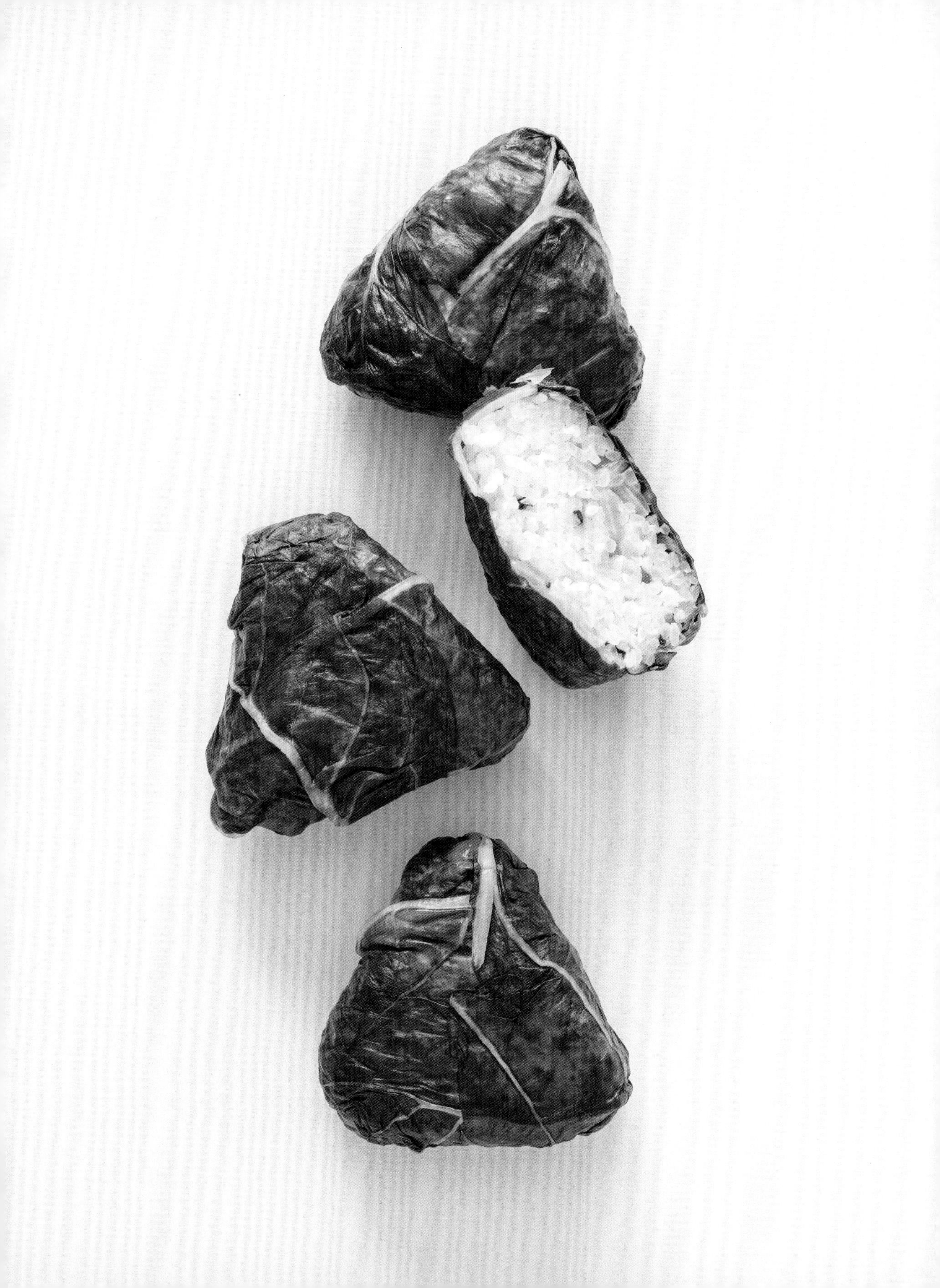

Kimchi nattō

⬤ × 6

1½ cups rice

About ½ cup vegan kimchi

**1 pack (¼ cup) *nattō*
(fermented soybeans)**

2 teaspoons soy sauce

***Nori* seaweed, for assembly**

STEPS

Cook your rice (see page 12) and let it cool.

Chop and then drain the kimchi.

Mix the *nattō*, soy sauce, and kimchi in a bowl.

Cover a cutting board with a bit of plastic wrap and place some rice on top. Create a triangle shape with the rice, place the *nattō* mixture in the center of the rice, and cover with the same amount of rice.

Cover entirely with the plastic wrap and delicately shape your onigiri. Wrap the *nori* around the onigiri so it keeps its shape.

Since *nattō* is a viscous ingredient, there's a risk of it sliding out of your onigiri if you press too hard, so be careful to gently wrap it when shaping. Just like miso, *nattō* is a product of the fermentation of soy that Japanese people love. Nattokinase, a protein found in *nattō*, is a blood thinner and is said to be effective at preventing vascular diseases. Furthermore, mixing *nattō* and kimchi is said to multiply the positive effect on the body because the oligosaccharides found in *nattō* nourish themselves with the lactic bacteria found in kimchi, thus allowing for improved bowel regulation.

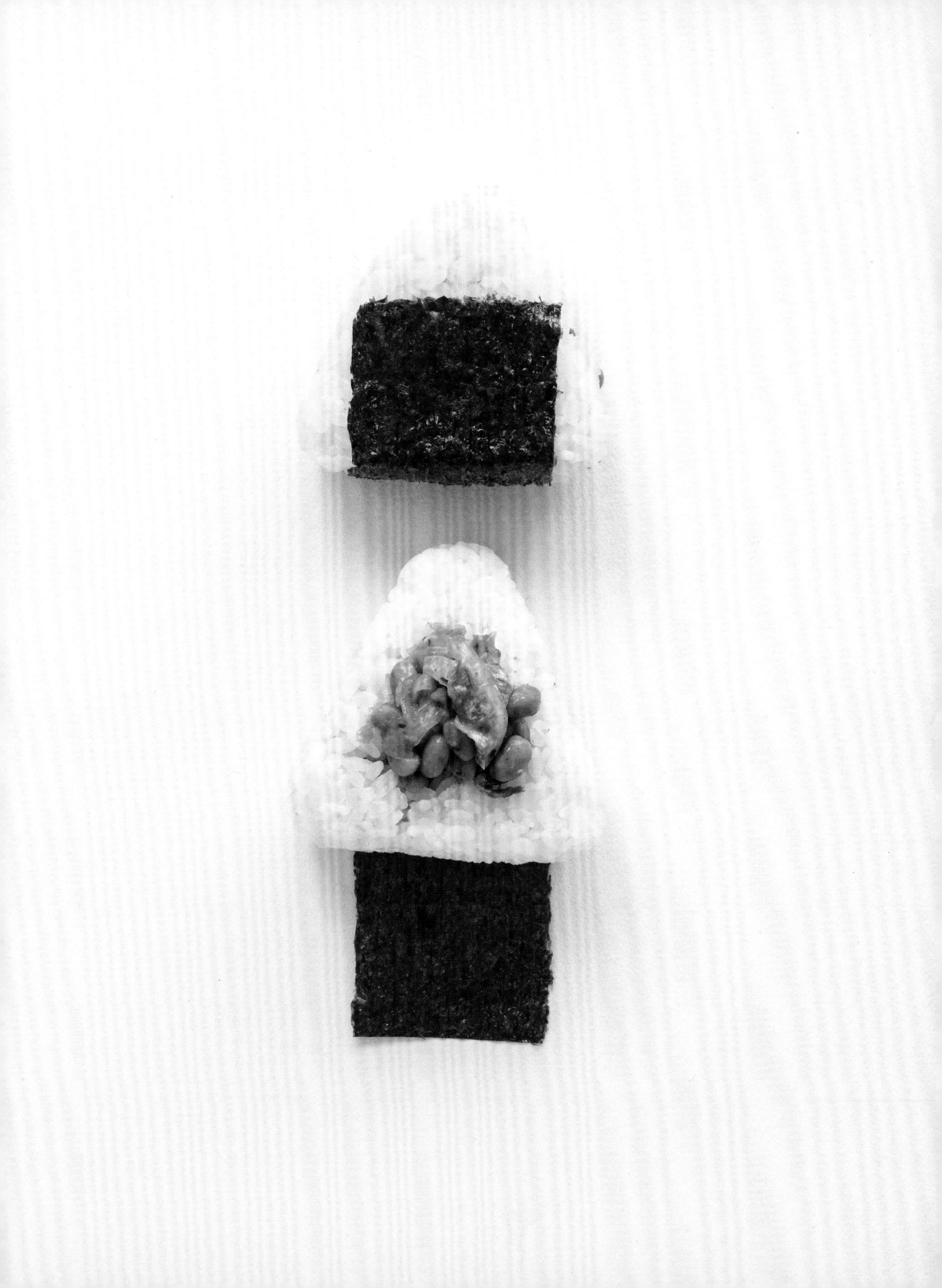

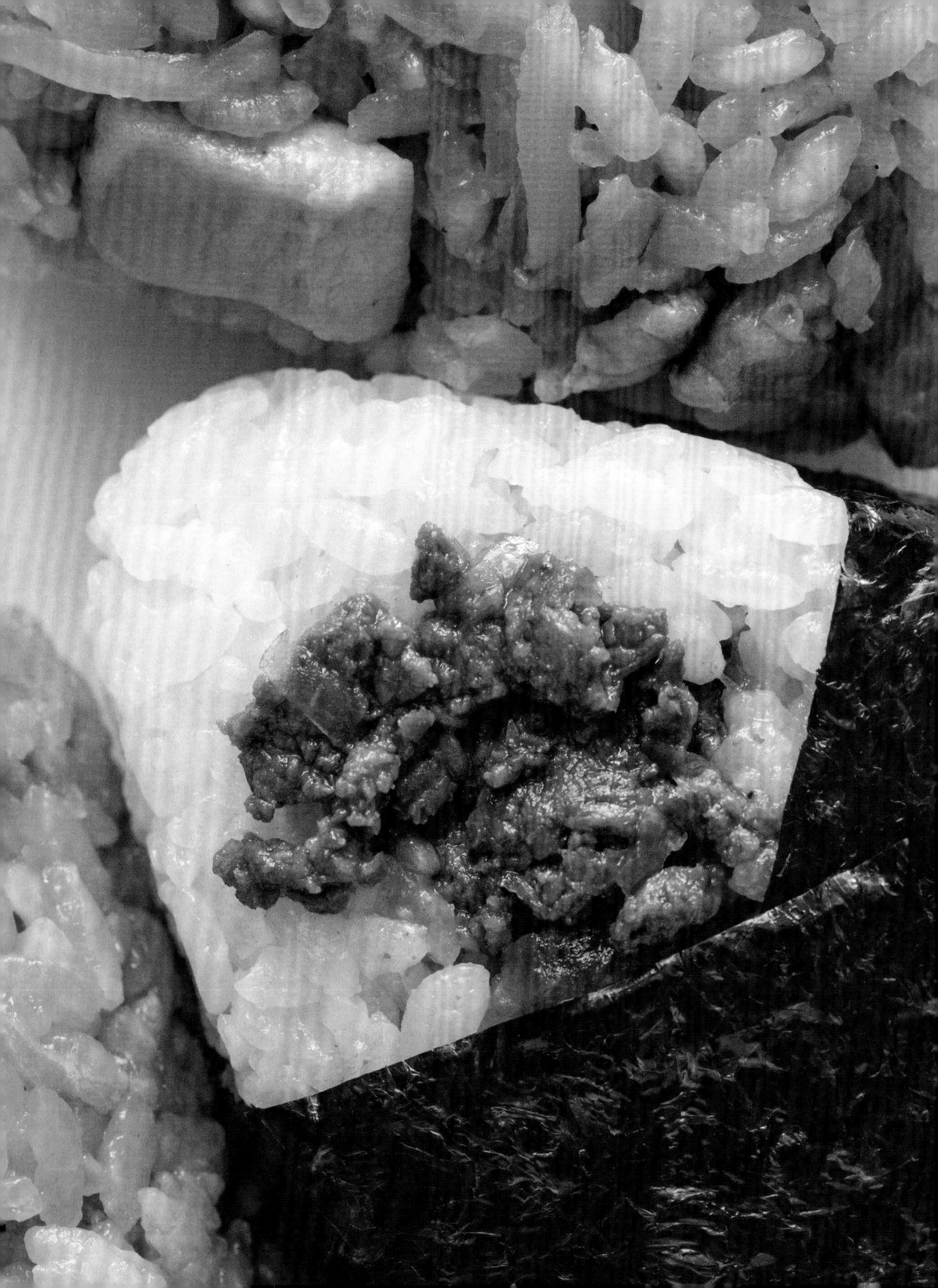

Meat

Chanterelle omelet

⬤ × 6

1½ cups rice

3½ ounces fresh *chanterelle* mushrooms

⅓ ounce unsalted butter (add salt to taste)

1 clove garlic, minced

2 eggs

1 teaspoon parsley, chopped

Salt and pepper, to taste

STEPS

Cook your rice (see page 12) and let it cool.

Wash the mushrooms using a damp paper towel. Cut off the base of the mushrooms, and add a small notch to the caps.

Melt the butter in a frying pan over low heat. Panfry the garlic for 1 minute, or until it releases its aroma. Add the mushrooms and sauté for 8–10 minutes, until their juices evaporate.

Beat the eggs in a small bowl, and add to the pan, raising the heat to medium. Carefully stir with a spatula to make slightly scrambled eggs.

Sprinkle the parsley on top of the eggs, add salt and pepper to taste, and turn off the heat before the eggs are fully cooked.

Grab a salad bowl and carefully mix the garnish and rice. Shape your onigiri.

To make your eggs light and airy, cook them while stirring quickly but gently, and keep them in the center of the frying pan. To prevent your eggs from sticking to the pan, add a bit more butter or use a nonstick frying pan.

Eggs

🍙 × 6

3 eggs

1½ cups rice

3 tablespoons soy sauce

3 tablespoons *mirin*

Chives, to taste

Sesame seeds, to taste

STEPS

Place the eggs in a container and put them in the freezer overnight.

Once the eggs are frozen, break their shells and peel them under cold water. Place the eggs in a clean container and let them thaw in your refrigerator.

Cook your rice (see page 12) and let it cool.

Separate the yolks from the egg whites, cut them in half, and place the yolks in a bowl with the soy sauce and *mirin* for at least half a day. Be sure to turn them over about halfway through marinating so the marinade is evenly absorbed by the yolks.

Sprinkle the yolks with the chives and sesame seeds to taste. Place the yolks in the middle of your onigiri and shape.

This is a delicious and addictive recipe. These onigiri are a perfect appetizer and will pair well with a glass of your favorite alcoholic beverage. Since the egg yolks aren't cooked, it is not recommended to pack these to eat on the go. Be aware that consumption of raw eggs may increase your risk of food-borne illness and take care when preparing this dish.

Garlic pork

⬤ × 6

STEPS

1½ cups rice

5⅓ ounces pork belly, sliced

1 teaspoon salt

1 teaspoon pepper

Up to 2 tablespoons wheat flour or potato starch

Oil, for cooking

2½ ounces spring onions

1 clove garlic, finely grated

1 tablespoon crushed sesame seeds

2 tablespoons grilled sesame seed oil

1½ teaspoons lemon juice

Cook your rice (see page 12) and let it cool.

Cut the pork belly into small portions. Season with salt and pepper, and coat with either the flour or starch.

Heat the oil in a frying pan over medium heat and cook the pork belly until the meat changes color. Flip the pieces and cook further for 2–3 minutes on each side.

Drain the pork on a plate lined with a paper towel. Add the remaining ingredients to the pan and mix to create a sauce. Coat the pieces of pork in the sauce.

Place the garnish in the middle of your onigiri and shape.

Be sure to wipe the pork belly with paper towels before seasoning to keep the flour from absorbing any excess humidity and producing a pasty mouthfeel. If you use flour, you will have a crispier final product. If you use starch, your sauce will be thicker, allowing it to better coat the meat. In either case, do not forget to pat the meat after cooking to remove any excess fluids.

Bacon and asparagus

🍙 × 6

1½ **cups rice**

6 large green asparagus

4 thin slices smoked bacon

Salt and pepper, to taste

STEPS

Cook your rice (see page 12) and let it cool.

Cut off the lower 2–3 inches of asparagus (the part that is hard and is white or purple). Peel the stems using a peeler, and then cut the asparagus in half crosswise, making 12 pieces.

Cut the smoked bacon slices in half and wrap every half around 2 asparagus pieces.

Place a frying pan over medium heat and put the rolls with the bacon wrap facing down into the pan. Cook for 2 minutes, until the side has slightly changed color, and then flip, cooking the second side for the same amount of time. Reduce the heat to low, cover, and leave the rolls in the pan for another 2–3 minutes. Season lightly with salt and pepper to taste, then remove from heat.

Place the rolls standing up in the middle of the onigiri and shape so the tops of the asparagus slightly peek out.

If you would like to try another version of this recipe, you can cut the asparagus in pieces and shape the mixed onigiri using the bacon instead of the *nori*. You can also make sushi-style rolls by wrapping the asparagus in rice, then rolling it in bacon.

Gyūdon

🍙 × 6

1½ **cups rice**

⅓ **cup onions**

⅓ **pound ground beef**

2 **tablespoons soy sauce**

1 **tablespoon sake**

1 **tablespoon** *mirin*

1 **tablespoon sugar**

⅓ **ounce grated ginger**

STEPS

Cook your rice (see page 12) and let it cool.

Chop the onion into *brunoise*, and sauté in a pan over medium heat for 2–3 minutes.

Add the ground beef and cook for 4–5 minutes, until it browns.

Pour in the soy sauce, sake, *mirin*, and sugar, and cook until the sauce has slightly reduced, roughly 1 minute. Mix in the grated ginger.

Place the garnish in the middle of your onigiri and shape.

If you are not able to digest gluten, you can use tamari sauce instead of soy sauce. Tamari sauce is made without any cereals or other additives.

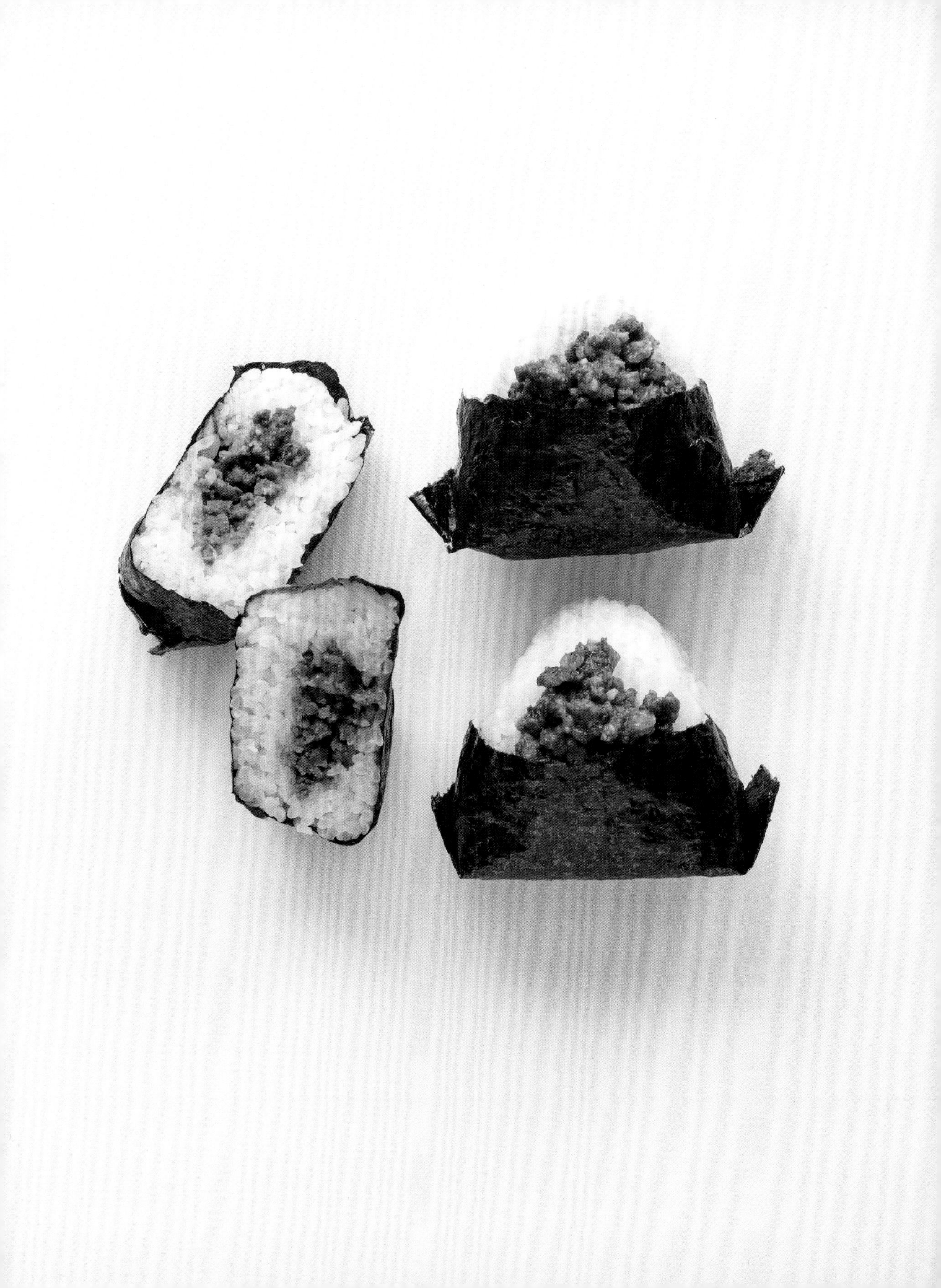

Duck breast

Chef Olivier Valade of the Château Saint-Jean in Montluçon, France

⌂ × 10

- **1½ cups rice**
- **2 tablespoons plus 2 teaspoons soy sauce**
- **2 tablespoons red miso**
- **1 tablespoon plus 1 teaspoon sesame oil**
- **¼ pomelo**
- **2 teaspoons Calamansi vinegar (or rice vinegar with a squeeze of tangerine/lime)**
- **1 pressed duck breast, skin on**
- **0.14 ounces sesame and *nori furikake***

STEPS

Cook your rice (see page 12) and let it cool.

Prepare the marinade. Mix the soy sauce, miso, sesame oil, a squeeze of pomelo juice, and the Calamansi vinegar in a bowl.

Score the duck fillet skin all the way to the flesh in a grid pattern. Brown the skin in a pan for 6–8 minutes, until it turns crispy.

Flip the fillet and let it cook for 6–7 minutes over low heat.

While hot, baste the fillet with the marinade, move it to a plate to cool slightly, and then wrap it tightly in plastic wrap. Store in the refrigerator for at least 24 hours.

Peel the remaining pomelo. Remove the white pith around the pulp, keeping only the pulp.

Cut the duck fillet into small pieces, in the range of ½–⅛ inch. Return the pieces to the bowl with a portion of the remaining marinade (to taste), and mix in the pomelo pulp and the *furikake*.

Garnish your onigiri.

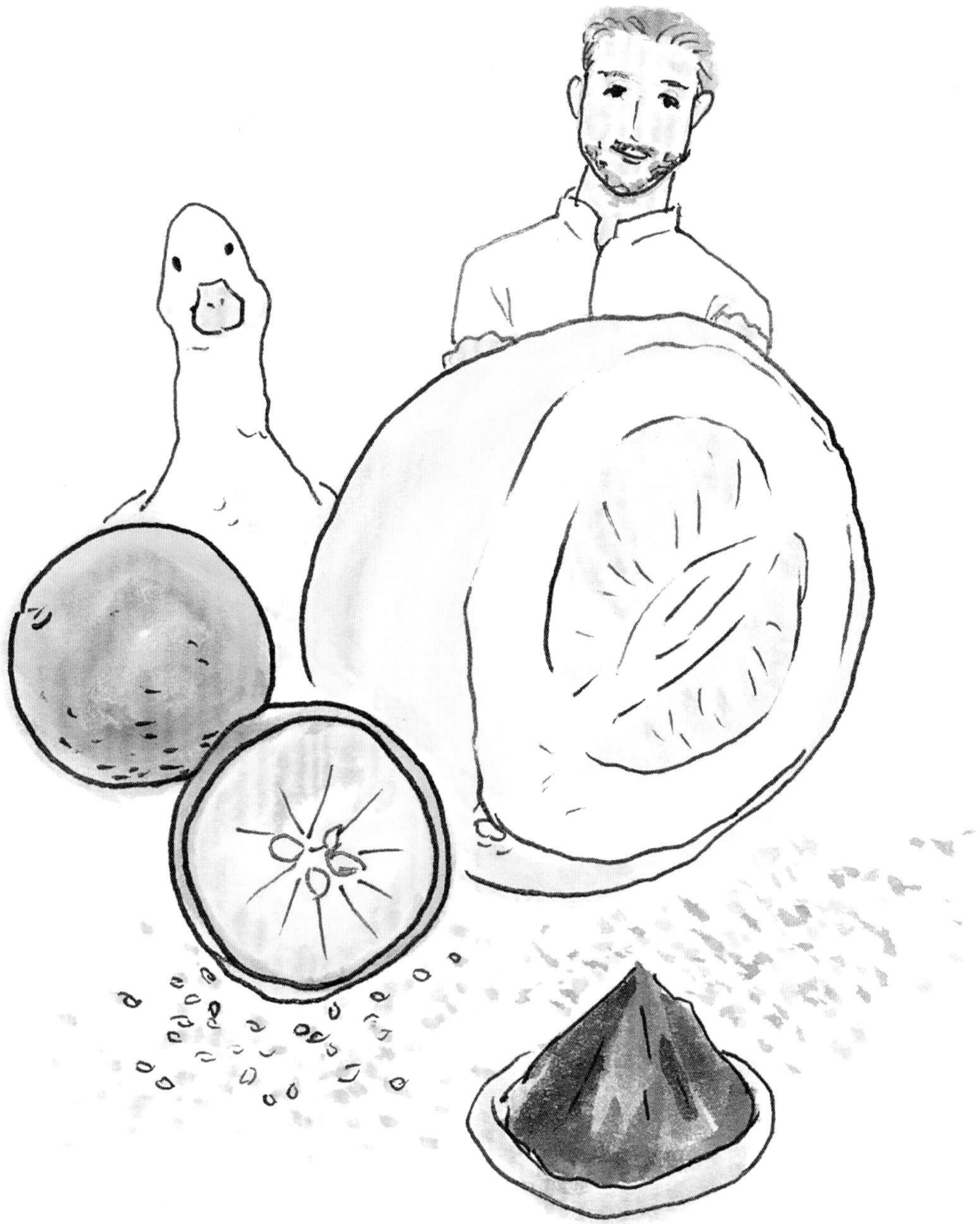

Ume and ponzu chicken

🍙 × 6

1½ cups rice

1 inch ginger

1 thinly cut slice chicken
   breast

2 *umeboshi*
   (about ⅔ ounce)

1 tablespoon ponzu

Sesame seeds, to taste

Spring onions, chopped,
   to taste

STEPS

Cook your rice (see page 12) and let it cool.

Bring a pot of around 2 cups of water to boil. Peel and immerse the ginger in the boiling water. Add the chicken, and once the water starts boiling again, cook for 1 minute before removing the pot from the heat. Let the chicken poach by keeping it in the pot for about 15 more minutes.

While the chicken is cooking, pit the *umeboshi* and crush them. Roughly mix the *umeboshi* with the ponzu in a bowl.

Drain the chicken, then dry and shred it. Take the chicken and mix it into the ponzu and *umeboshi* mixture. Finally, sprinkle with the sesame seeds and onions to taste.

Place the garnish in the middle of your onigiri and shape.

The highly antiseptic *umeboshi* has always been an important onigiri garnish. *Umeboshi* is usually pickled and sour, but it also comes in other varieties: sweet and sour seasoned with honey or even crunchy when made from young plums. Its acidity and salt content depend on the producer. Be sure to taste test the dish to balance out the flavors. When I made this recipe, I used a very sour type of *umeboshi*.

Grilled Comté cheese

⊙ × 6

1½ cups rice

1¾ ounces shredded Comté cheese

1⅛ ounces white miso

2 tablespoons *mirin*

2 teaspoons sugar

Scallions, to taste

***Shichimi togarashi*, to taste**

STEPS

Cook your rice (see page 12) and let it cool.

Divide your shredded Comté cheese into six piles of roughly equal proportions.

Shape your onigiri with the cheese in the center *without* rubbing salt on your hands. Firmly press on the rice as you shape the onigiri.

Put a sheet of parchment paper in a frying pan, place the onigiri on top, and raise the heat to medium. Cook for 6–8 minutes while regularly turning the onigiri over until both sides become an appealing color.

Mix the miso, *mirin*, and sugar in a bowl. Brush one side of the onigiri with the mixture, then grill that side for 2 minutes. Remove the onigiri from the heat and add some scallions and *shichimi* to taste.

Make sure you put a lot of pressure on the rice when shaping the onigiri so they don't fall apart when turning them over in the frying pan. Also avoid raising the heat too much, as the miso sauce tends to burn easily.

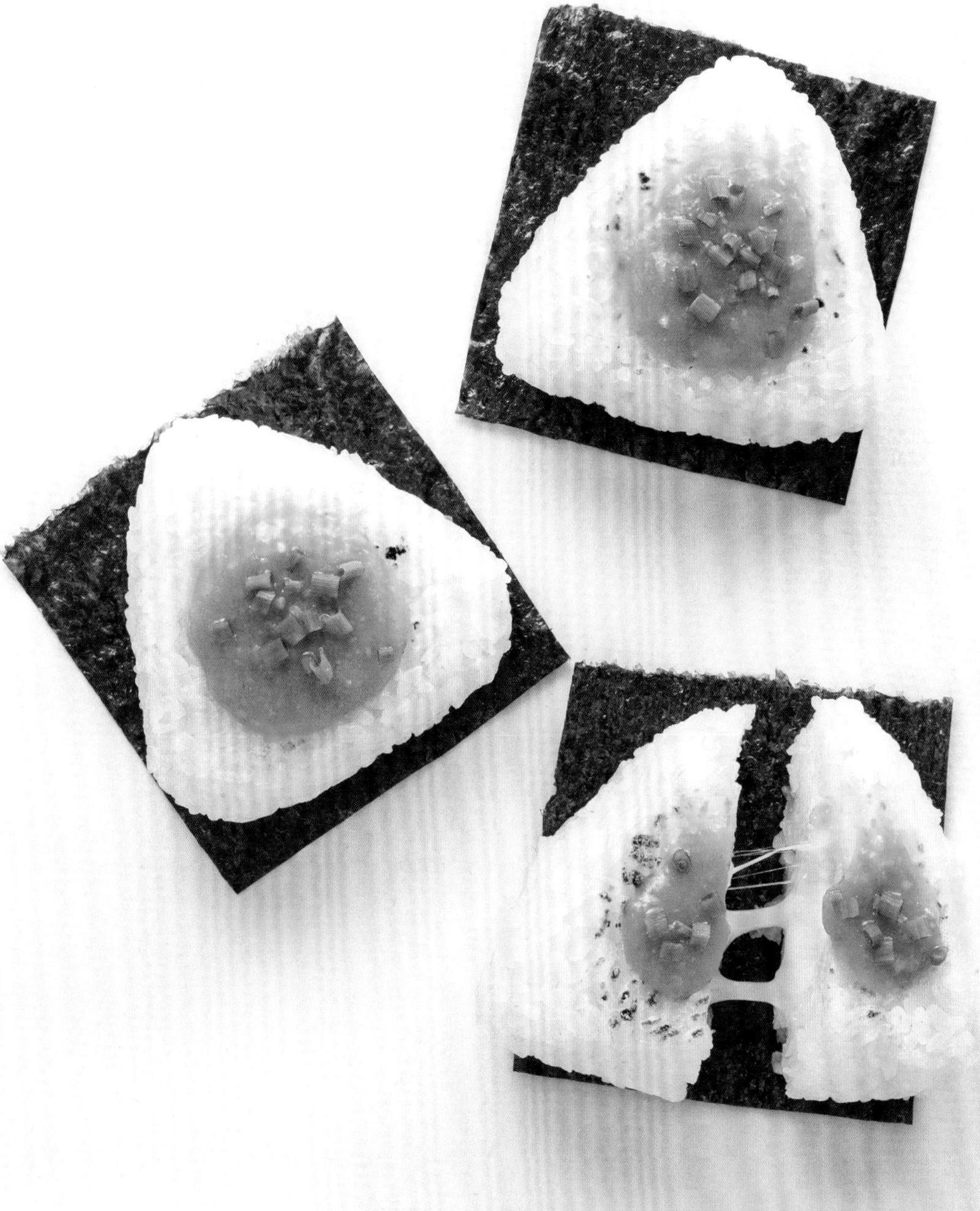

Torimeshi

🍙 × 6

7 ounces boneless chicken thighs

2½ ounces Jerusalem artichokes, julienned

2½ ounces carrots, julienned

2 cloves garlic, grated

4 tablespoons soy sauce

2 tablespoons sake

2 teaspoons sugar

1½ cups rice

STEPS

Remove the skin from the chicken and cut the skin into small pieces. Soak the julienned artichokes in water for about 10 minutes.

Heat the chicken skin in a pan for 3–4 minutes until it secretes enough grease, and discard the grease. Remove the skin and then sauté the pieces of chicken on medium heat. Add the drained artichokes and julienned carrots, and continue cooking.

Combine the garlic, soy sauce, sake, and sugar in a bowl. Pour the sauce over the chicken, and reduce the sauce by about a third over low heat, stirring constantly. You can gauge the progress by tilting the pan and looking at the liquid that gathers.

Cook the rice. Once cooked, immediately add the garnish to the pot, stir, cover, and let sit for 10 minutes. Shape your onigiri.

This technique is also known as *mazekomi* in Japanese. It means to cook the rice and then add the sauce and should not be confused with the *takikomi* technique, where the sauce is added during the cooking process.

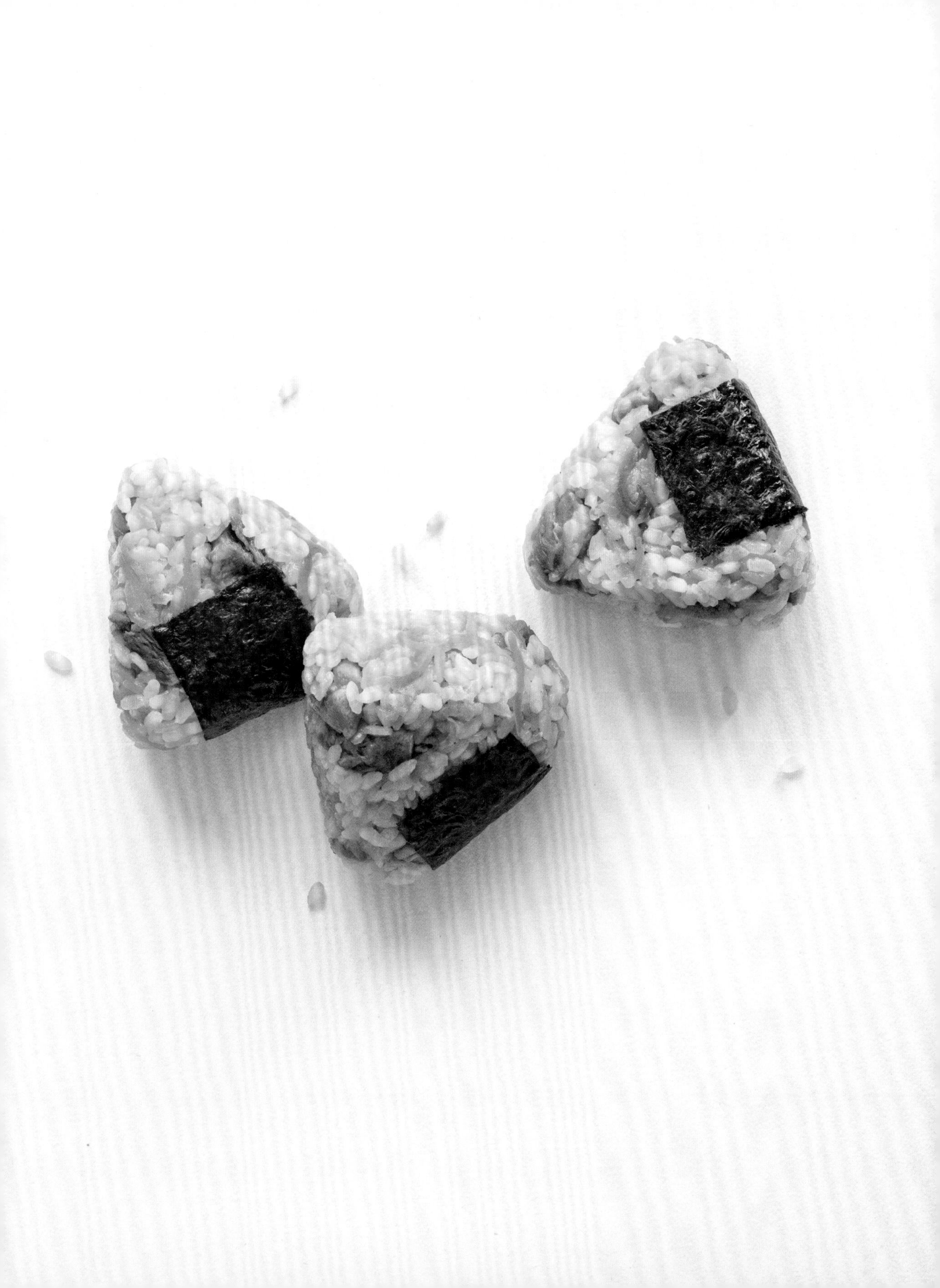

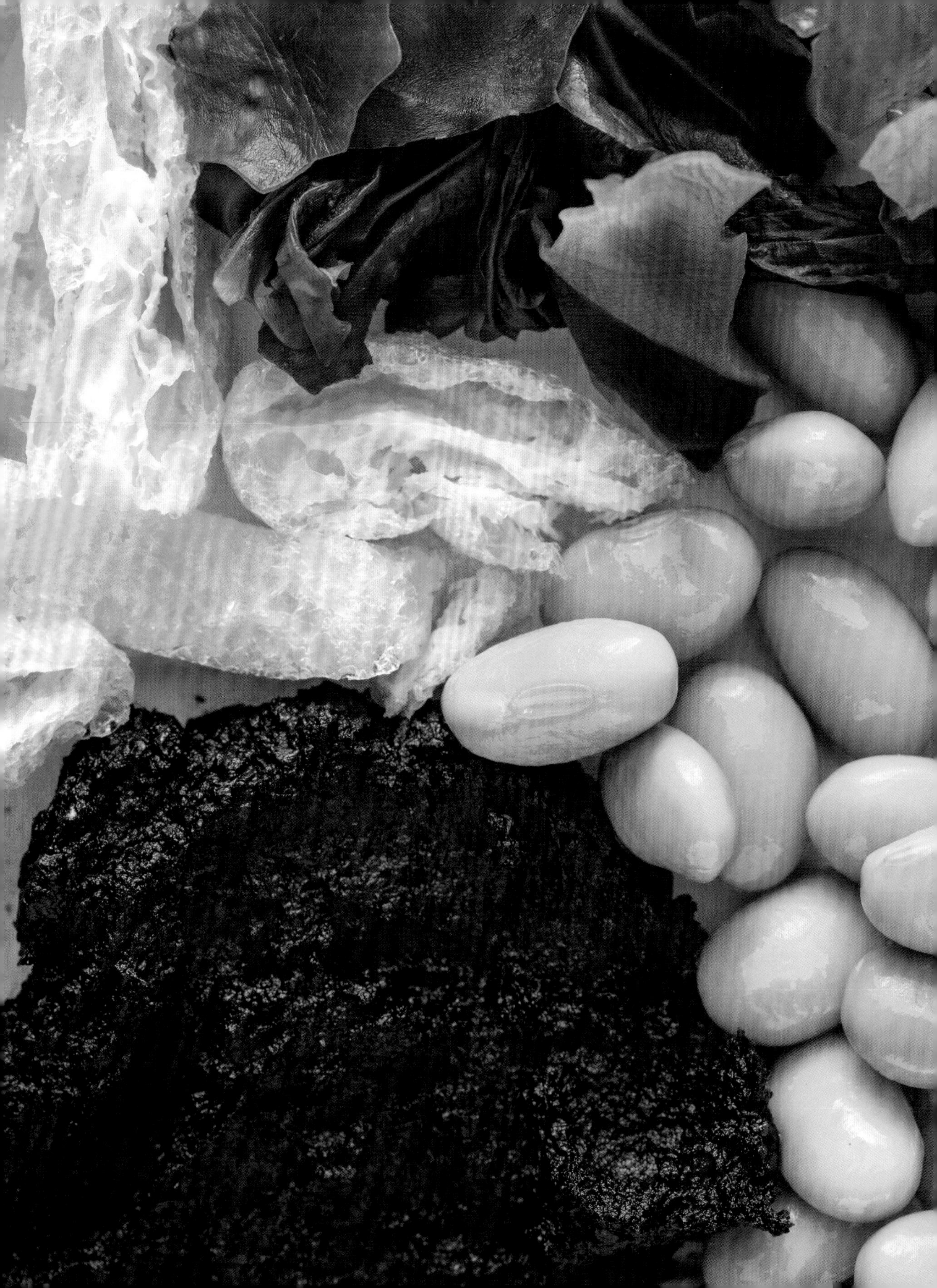

Soup, Snacks & Pickled Food

Miso soup

🍙 × 2

4 teaspoons dried
  wakame seaweed

¼ block firm tofu

1 pint water

1 cup dried bonito
  flakes, packed

¼ cup spring onion,
  chopped

1 tablespoon miso

STEPS

Soak the dried *wakame* seaweed in water for 5 minutes, and then drain thoroughly.

Cut the tofu into roughly ¾-inch cubes.

Bring the pint of water to a boil in a pan, and add the dried bonito flakes. Let them boil for about 3 minutes or until the bonito is entirely submerged, then turn off the heat.

Use a colander covered with paper towels to filter the bouillon, preserving the liquid.

Return the filtered bouillon to the pan and put back on the stove.

Add the *wakame*, tofu, and spring onions, and let the mixture cook until it starts bubbling.

Add the miso and stir until it is completely dissolved. Then remove the pan from the heat (do not let the soup boil) and serve.

Cream of mushroom soup

🍙 × 2

4-by-4-inch square of dried *kombu* kelp

¾ cup plus 2½ teaspoons water

1 ounce *shimeji* mushrooms

1 ounce *maitake* mushrooms

1 ounce *shiitake* mushrooms

1¾ ounces onions

1¾ ounces sweet potatoes

1¼ cup and 1 teaspoon of unsweetened, plain soy milk

1 teaspoon soy sauce

1 tablespoon miso

Scallion, chopped, for garnishing

Pepper, for garnishing

STEPS

Let the *kombu* soak in water for 30 minutes.

Chop off the bases of the *shimeji* and *maitake* mushrooms and separate them. Slice the *shiitake* mushrooms and onions into strips. Peel the sweet potatoes and cut in paysanne. Let them soak in water for 5 minutes.

Heat up some water in a pan with the *kombu* to make a broth. Bring to a boil and then remove the *kombu* after 1 minute. Add the mushrooms, onions, and sweet potatoes, and cook until the sweet potatoes become soft.

Add the soy milk and soy sauce to the pan. Be sure not to let the mixture get past 145°F (63°C), so the soup doesn't curdle.

Once the soup is hot, add the miso. Once it is dissolved in the soup, remove the pan from the heat.

Pour the soup in bowls, and add the chopped scallion and pepper.

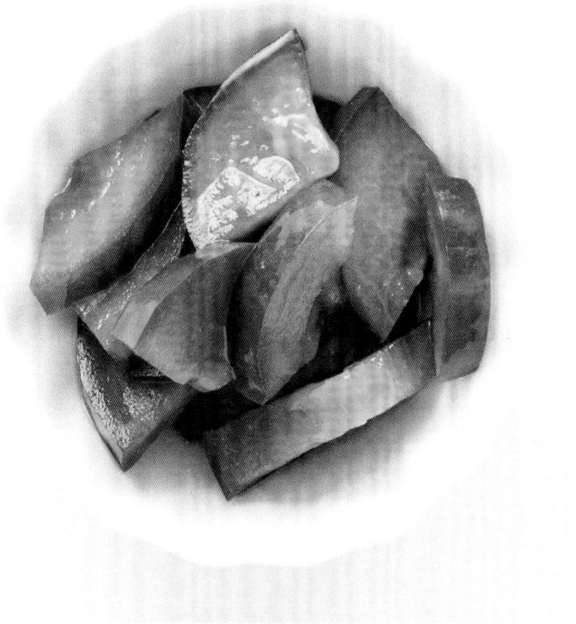

PICKLED

Pickled cucumber

1 cucumber

1 tablespoon plus 1 teaspoon coarse salt

10 tablespoons soy sauce

2 tablespoons vinegar

1 tablespoon *mirin*

¼ cup sugar

¼ cup ginger, julienned

1 tablespoon chili powder

STEPS

Wash the cucumber, and then rub it with 1 teaspoon of salt and let it penetrate. Rinse the cucumber and cut into slices about 8 millimeters thick, and then quarter those slices.

Roughly mix the tablespoon of coarse salt with the cucumber in a bowl. Place in the refrigerator and let it sweat for 30 minutes.

Heat the soy sauce, vinegar, *mirin*, sugar, peeled and julienned ginger, and chili powder in a pan. Bring to a boil to let the alcohol from the *mirin* evaporate. Before adding the cucumber pieces to the pan, squeeze them to remove any excess water. After the cucumbers are added, quickly remove the pan from the heat and let the mixture cool.

Once cooled, remove the cucumber pieces and bring the marinade to a boil. Once boiling, remove from heat, and quickly dip the cucumber pieces into the marinade. Repeat this dipping process twice.

This pickled dish can be kept for up to 3 weeks in the refrigerator.

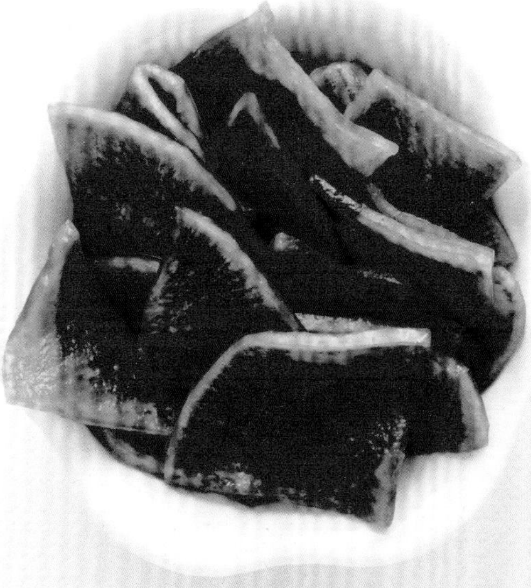

PICKLED

Pickled radish

Around 14 ounces daikon radish

1 tablespoon coarse salt

1 tablespoon rice vinegar

4 tablespoons sugar

2-by-2-inch square of *kombu*

20 grams dried yuzu lemon zest

1 tablespoon yuzu lemon juice

STEPS

Peel the daikon radish and cut it into paysanne, then quarter it.

Mix the daikon pieces with the coarse salt in a bowl. Cover the bowl and weigh down the cover. Place in the refrigerator, and let it sweat for 1 hour.

Squeeze the daikon to remove any excess water and then mix it with the vinegar, sugar, *kombu*, and yuzu (both the zest and juice) in a freezer bag. Massage it.

Let it marinate for at least 12 hours in the refrigerator before serving.

This pickled dish can be kept for up to 10 days in the refrigerator.

GUEST

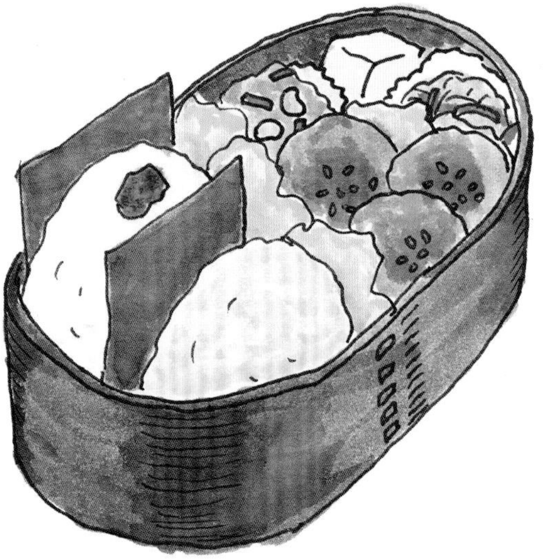

Chef Shigeaki Yoshi of Onigiri Café Risaku in Sendagi, Tokyo, Japan

Just over ¼ pound ground chicken

Just over 1 teaspoon miso

½ teaspoon sake

1 teaspoon clear soy sauce

1 small egg

1 tablespoon plus 1 teaspoon lotus root, diced

½ ounce onions

2 tablespoons plus 2 teaspoons plain breadcrumbs

1 teaspoon potato starch

2 tablespoons dark soy sauce

1 tablespoon *mirin*

1 tablespoon sake

1 tablespoon powdered sugar

1 scallion greens

½ inch ginger, peeled and sliced

Chicken tsukune

STEPS

Mix the chicken with the miso, sake, and clear soy sauce in a bowl. Massage well to keep the meat from splitting during the cooking process and to lock in the juices. Beat the egg and add 1 ounce of it to the mix. Dice and add the lotus root, and then introduce the egg, onions, bread crumbs, and starch, in that order. Form the meatballs and size to taste.

Place the meatballs in a pan over medium heat, and cook for 4–5 minutes until browned. Reduce the heat to low, and add the dark soy sauce, *mirin*, sake, powdered sugar, scallion greens, and ginger. Cover and cook until the sugar has dissolved and the sauce thickens.

This sauce can be used as a teriyaki sauce or as the basis for a *mizoreni,* a dish consisting of meat or fish served in a broth and garnished with grated daikon radish. If you wanted to make *mizoreni,* just dilute the sauce with water and add the daikon radish.

Chicken contains vitamin A and is much leaner than beef or pork (even minced, it has half the fat content). To make *tsukune*, Café Risaku uses *Ōyama* chicken, a type of chicken raised at the foot of the mountains in Tottori Prefecture.

GUEST

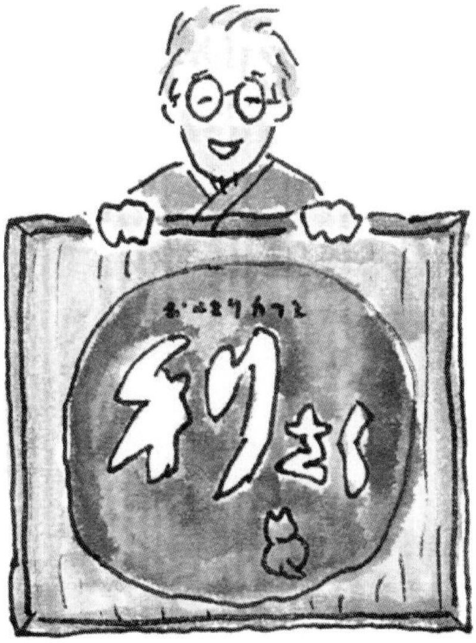

Chef Shigeaki Yoshi of Onigiri Café Risaku in Sendagi, Tokyo, Japan

Dashimaki eggs

¼ cup *katsuodashi* (*dashi* broth made from dried bonito)

1 teaspoon soy sauce

2 teaspoons sugar

2 eggs

Oil

STEPS

Heat the *katsuodashi* in a pan along with the soy sauce and sugar. Once the sugar has dissolved, move the mixture to a container and let it cool. Crack and add the eggs to the mixture.

Place a small pan over medium heat. Add a dash of oil to the pan, and pour in about half of your mixture. Once the eggs start cooking, gently mix with a pair of chopsticks so they cook evenly. Roll the omelet to the front of the pan before it is finished cooking.

Move the omelet to the opposite side of the pan, and add another ⅓ of your mixture. Be sure to gently lift your first layer so the second can spread underneath. Cook this portion the same way as described in the previous step. Repeat the cooking process with the last portion of the mixture as well.

This may remind you of an omelet, but unlike an omelet, the *dashimaki* should be well-done and not runny. In Japanese cooking, the broth would of course be *kombu* or bonito *dashi*, but you can create this dish the same way using vegetable bouillon.

Map of Tokyo

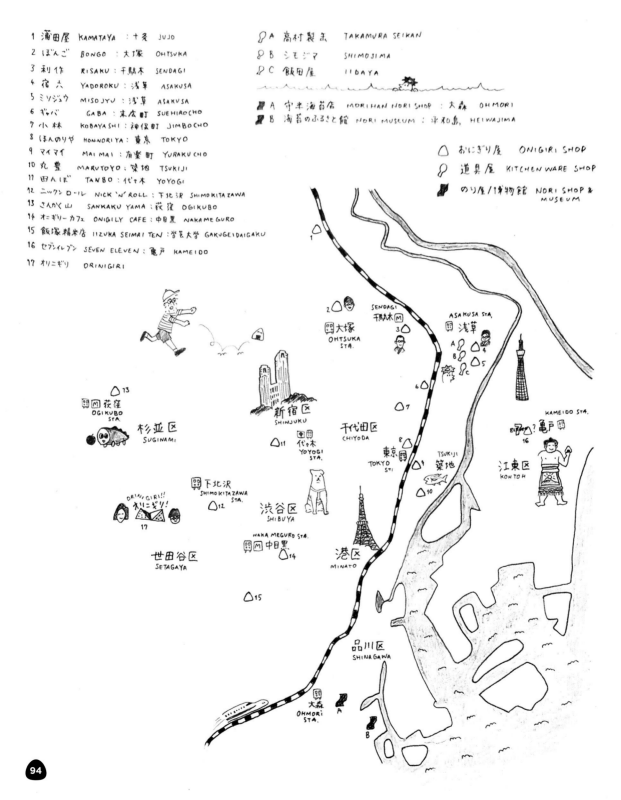

1 蒲田屋 KAMATAYA : 十条 JUJO
2 ぼんご BONGO : 大塚 OHTSUKA
3 利作 RISAKU : 千駄木 SENDAGI
4 宿六 YADOROKU : 浅草 ASAKUSA
5 ミソジュウ MISOJYU : 浅草 ASAKUSA
6 ギャバ GABA : 末広町 SUEHIROCHO
7 小林 KOBAYASHI : 神保町 JIMBOCHO
8 ほんのりや HONNORIYA : 東京 TOKYO
9 マイマイ MAIMAI : 有楽町 YURAKUCHO
10 丸豊 MARUTOYO : 築地 TSUKIJI
11 田んぼ TANBO : 代々木 YOYOGI
12 ニックンロール NICK 'N' ROLL : 下北沢 SHIMOKITAZAWA
13 さんかく山 SANKAKU YAMA : 荻窪 OGIKUBO
14 オニギリーカフェ ONIGILY CAFE : 中目黒 NAKAMEGURO
15 飯塚精米店 IIZUKA SEIMAI TEN : 学芸大学 GAKUGEIDAIGAKU
16 セブンイレブン SEVEN ELEVEN : 亀戸 KAMEIDO
17 オリニギリ ORINIGIRI

A 高村製缶 TAKAMURA SEIKAN
B シモジマ SHIMOJIMA
C 飯田屋 IIDAYA

A 守半海苔店 MORIHAN NORI SHOP : 大森 OHMORI
B 海苔のふるさと館 NORI MUSEUM : 平和島 HEIWAJIMA

おにぎり屋 ONIGIRI SHOP
道具屋 KITCHENWARE SHOP
のり屋/博物館 NORI SHOP & MUSEUM

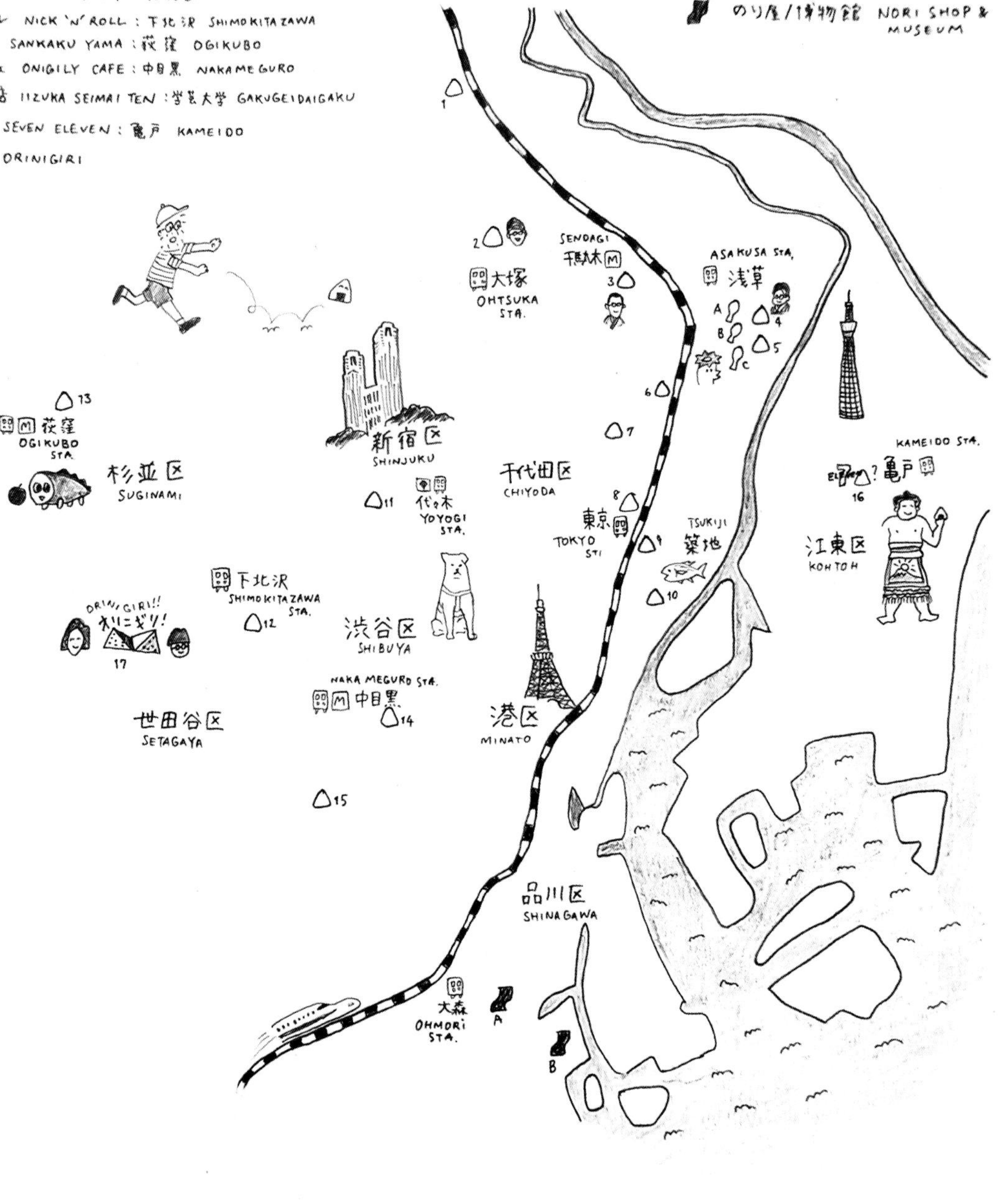

SENDAGI
千駄木
大塚
OHTSUKA STA.
ASAKUSA STA.
浅草
荻窪
OGIKUBO STA.
杉並区
SUGINAMI
新宿区
SHINJUKU
代々木
YOYOGI STA.
千代田区
CHIYODA
東京
TOKYO STA.
TSUKIJI
築地
KAMEIDO STA.
亀戸
江東区
KOHTOH
下北沢
SHIMOKITAZAWA STA.
ORINIGIRI!!
オリニギリ!
渋谷区
SHIBUYA
NAKA MEGURO STA.
中目黒
世田谷区
SETAGAYA
港区
MINATO
品川区
SHINAGAWA
大森
OHMORI STA.

Index

Special thanks

Thank you to our families—Chiyomi, Katsue, Isao, Yuki, Mariko, Lee, Noah, Kayo, Asami, Maria, Mika, Pascaline, Alain, Marion, Jonas, Christine, Michel, Michiko, Haruka—and to our friends.

We would also like to thank all our MiiMOSA crowdfunding backers, our customers, our suppliers, the French Rice Center, the Le Renard Doré bookstore in Paris, the Paris Aquarium, the Tokyo onigiri restaurants we consulted and were inspired by, the TV Tokyo and Nippon TV team, Caroline de Maigret, Vincent Desclaux, and Jonathan Noblet.

Useful information

Here's a list of ingredients that are essential to creating your onigiri: short-grain rice, dried black seaweed (nori), soy sauce, Japanese *mirin* rice wine, sake, sesame seeds, toasted sesame oil, wasabi, dried green laver (*aonori*), rice and soy miso, *abura-age*, dried bonito flakes (*katsuobushi*), and *nattō*.

All the ingredients you may need to create a beautiful and tasty onigiri can be found at your local Asian or Japanese grocery store.

We also prepared a map (see page 94) with some useful locations in Tokyo.

Onigiri

BY AI WATANABE & SAMUEL TRIFOT

VIZ Media
TRANSLATION: (·∀·`)ｻﾌ?
DESIGN: Francesca Truman
RECIPE TESTING: Jenn de la Vega
EDITOR: David Brothers

Editions First
COORDINATION: Samuel Trifot
PHOTOGRAPHY: Akiko Ida
ILLUSTRATIONS: Ai Watanabe
JAPANESE TEXT TRANSLATIONS:
Yumena Miyanaga
GRAPHIC CONCEPT: Vincent Desclaux
LAYOUTS: Transparence
PROOFREADING: Natacha Kotchetkova
CORRECTIONS: Véronique Dussidour

©Editions First, an imprint of Edi8, 2022

Printed in China

Library of Congress Control Number: 2021948552

Published by VIZ Media, LLC
P.O. Box 77010
San Francisco, CA 94107

10 9 8 7 6 5 4 3 2 1
First printing, April 2022

VIZ MEDIA
viz.com

If you happen to pass through Paris, we'll be awaiting your visit to our shop on 48 rue Notre Dame de Lorette!

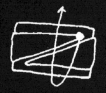

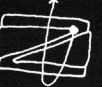